Fremdsprachentexte

an
ps

Herausgegeben von
Christopher Harvie

Philipp Reclam jun. Stuttgart

Diese Ausgabe darf nur in der Bundesrepublik Deutschland, in Österreich und in der Schweiz vertrieben werden.

Universal-Bibliothek Nr. 9051

Umschlagabbildung: Szenenphoto aus der Verfilmung von Alfred Hitchcock (England 1935)
Gesamtherstellung: Reclam, Ditzingen. Printed in Germany 1998
RECLAM und UNIVERSAL-BIBLIOTHEK sind eingetragene Marken der Philipp Reclam jun. GmbH & Co., Stuttgart
ISBN 3-15-009051-2

The Thirty-Nine Steps

To

THOMAS ARTHUR NELSON
(LOTHIAN AND BORDER HORSE)

My Dear Tommy,

You and I have long cherished an affection for that elementary type of tale which Americans call the "dime novel" and which we know as the "shocker" – the romance where the incidents defy the probabilities, and march just inside the borders of the possible. During an illness last winter I exhausted my store of those aids to cheerfulness, and was driven to write one for myself. This little volume is the result, and I should like to put your name on it in memory of our long friendship, in the days when the wildest fictions are so much less improbable than the facts.

J. B.

2 **Nelson:** Thomas Arthur N. (1878–1916), Zeitgenosse John Buchans in Oxford.

3 **Lothian:** Region Schottlands um die Hauptstadt Edinburgh.
Border: *Borders* (pl.): Region Schottlands an der Grenze zu England.
horse (infml.): Angehöriger der Kavallerie.

5 **to cherish:** (Gefühl) hegen.

6 **dime novel:** Groschenroman.

7 **shocker** (infml.): Schocker; etwas, das schockt.

8 **to defy:** trotzen, sich widersetzen.

11 **volume:** (Buch-)Band.

Chapter I

The Man who Died

I returned from the City about three o'clock on that May afternoon pretty well disgusted with life. I had been three months in the Old Country, and was fed up with it. If anyone had told me a year ago that I would have been feeling like that I should have laughed at him; but there was the fact. The weather made me liverish, the talk of the ordinary Englishman made me sick, I couldn't get enough exercise, and the amusements of London seemed as flat as soda-water that has been standing in the sun. "Richard Hannay," I kept telling myself, "you have got into the wrong ditch, my friend, and you had better climb out."

It made me bite my lips to think of the plans I had been building up those last years in Buluwayo. I had got my pile – not one of the big ones, but good enough for me; and I had figured out all kinds of ways of enjoying myself. My father had brought me out from Scotland at the age of six, and I had never been home since; so

4 (*to be*) **disgusted with s.th.:** angewidert von etwas sein, Ekel über etwas empfinden.
5 **Old Country:** Bezeichnung für England.
5 f. **to be fed up with s.th.:** genug von etwas haben.
9 **liverish** (infml.): mürrisch.
13 **ditch:** Graben.
16 **Buluwayo:** Bulawajo, Stadt in Rhodesien (Simbabwe) im Süden Afrikas.
17 **pile** (infml.): Menge Geld, Vermögen.

England was a sort of Arabian Nights to me, and I counted on stopping there for the rest of my days.

But from the first I was disappointed with it. In about a week I was tired of seeing sights, and in less than a month I had had enough of restaurants and theatres and race-meetings. I had no real pal to go about with, which probably explains things. Plenty of people invited me to their houses, but they didn't seem much interested in me. They would fling me a question or two about South Africa, and then get on their own affairs. A lot of Imperialist ladies asked me to tea to meet schoolmasters from New Zealand and editors from Vancouver, and that was the dismalest business of all. Here was I, thirty-seven years old, sound in wind and limb, with enough money to have a good time, yawning my head off all day. I had just about settled to clear out and get back to the veld, for I was the best bored man in the United Kingdom.

That afternoon I had been worrying my brokers about investments to give my mind something to work on, and on my way home I turned into my club – rather a pot-house, which took in Colonial members. I had a

1 **Arabian Nights:** Tausendundeine Nacht.
6 **pal** (infml.): Freund(in), Kumpel.
9 **to fling:** zuwerfen.
11 **Imperialist:** imperialistisch, auf das britische Kolonialreich bezogen.
13 **Vancouver:** Stadt an der südlichen Westküste Kanadas.
dismal: düster, trüb, trostlos, bedrückend.
14 f. **sound in wind and limb:** kerngesund.
16 **to clear out:** verschwinden, sich verziehen.
17 **veld** (S. Afr.): Gras- und Buschland Südafrikas.
19 **broker:** Makler(in), Vermittler(in), Finanzberater(in).
22 **pot-house** (arch.): kleines Lokal.
Colonial: auf die britischen Kronkolonien bezogen.

long drink, and read the evening papers. They were full of the row in the Near East, and there was an article about Karolides, the Greek Premier. I rather fancied the chap. From all accounts he seemed the one big man in the show; and he played a straight game too, which was more than could be said for most of them. I gathered that they hated him pretty blackly in Berlin and Vienna, but that we were going to stick by him, and one paper said that he was the only barrier between Europe and Armageddon. I remember wondering if I could get a job in those parts. It struck me that Albania was the sort of place that might keep a man from yawning.

About six o'clock I went home, dressed, dined at the Café Royal, and turned into a music-hall. It was a silly show, all capering women and monkey-faced men, and I did not stay long. The night was fine and clear as I walked back to the flat I had hired near Portland Place.

2 **row** (infml.): Krach, Streit.
3 **Karolides:** Constantine K., fiktiver griechischer Premierminister, vermutl. basierend auf Eleutherios Venizelos, griechischer Premierminister 1910–15.
4 **chap** (infml.): Bursche, Kerl.
8 **Vienna:** Wien.
to stick by s.o. (infml.): zu jdm. halten.
10 **Armageddon:** *Har Megiddo:* Bergregion südöstlich von Jaffa (Haifa) in Palästina, wo nach der Bibel die letzte Schlacht am Tag des Jüngsten Gerichts stattfinden soll.
11 **Albania:** Albanien wurde durch die Balkankriege von der türkischen Vorherrschaft befreit, geriet dann aber in innere Konflikte.
14 **Café Royal:** Londoner Lokal mit gehobenem Niveau.
music-hall: Varieté(theater).
15 **to caper:** Kapriolen machen.
monkey-faced: äffisch, albern.
17 **Portland Place:** Straße im Zentrum Londons, wo Buchan zur Zeit der Abfassung des vorliegenden Romans wohnte.

The crowd surged past me on the pavements, busy and chattering, and I envied the people for having something to do. These shop-girls and clerks and dandies and policemen had some interest in life that kept them going. I gave half-a-crown to a beggar because I saw him yawn; he was a fellow-sufferer. At Oxford Circus I looked up into the spring sky and I made a vow. I would give the Old Country another day to fit me into something; if nothing happened, I would take the next boat for the Cape.

My flat was the first floor in a new block behind Langham Place. There was a common staircase, with a porter and a liftman at the entrance, but there was no restaurant or anything of that sort, and each flat was quite shut off from the others. I hate servants on the premises, so I had a fellow to look after me who came in by the day. He arrived before eight o'clock every morning and used to depart at seven, for I never dined at home.

1 **to surge:** drängen, strömen, sich wälzen.
2 **to chatter:** plappern, schwatzen.
3 **dandy:** Geck, Stutzer.
5 **half-a-crown:** frühere britische Münze; entspricht 12 ½ Pence der heutigen Währung.
6 **fellow-sufferer:** Leidensgenosse, -genossin.
Oxford Circus: Kreuzung von Oxford Street und Regent Street im Zentrum Londons.
7 **to make a vow:** ein Gelöbnis ablegen.
8 f. **to fit s.o. into s.th.:** jdn. in etwas unterbringen, für jdn. den richtigen Platz finden.
10 **the Cape:** Kap der Guten Hoffnung an der Südspitze Afrikas.
11 f. **Langham Place:** Adresse im Zentrum Londons beim nahegelegenen Portland Place.
15 f. **on the premises** (pl.): an Ort und Stelle, im Haus.

I was just fitting my key into the door when I noticed a man at my elbow. I had not seen him approach, and the sudden appearance made me start. He was a slim man, with a short brown beard and small, gimlety blue eyes. I recognized him as the occupant of a flat on the top floor, with whom I had passed the time of day on the stairs.

"Can I speak to you?" he said. "May I come in for a minute?" He was steadying his voice with an effort, and his hand was pawing my arm.

I got my door open and motioned him in. No sooner was he over the threshold than he made a dash for my back room, where I used to smoke and write my letters. Then he bolted back.

"Is the door locked?" he asked feverishly, and he fastened the chain with his own hand.

"I'm very sorry", he said humbly. "It's a mighty liberty, but you looked the kind of man who would understand. I've had you in my mind all this week when things got troublesome. Say, will you do me a good turn?"

"I'll listen to you", I said. "That's all I promise." I was getting worried by the antics of this nervous little chap.

4 f. **gimlety eyes:** stechende Augen; Luchsaugen.
5 **occupant:** Bewohner(in), Mieter(in).
10 **to paw:** tätscheln; befummeln.
11 **to motion s.o. in:** jdn. hereinwinken.
12 **threshold:** Türschwelle.
to make a dash for s.th.: auf etwas zustürzen.
14 **to bolt back:** einen Satz zurück machen.
20 **troublesome:** lästig.
to do s.o. a good turn: jdm. einen guten Dienst erweisen.
22 **antics** (pl.): Possen, Mätzchen.

There was a tray of drinks on a table beside him, from which he filled himself a stiff whisky-and-soda. He drank it off in three gulps, and cracked the glass as he set it down.

"Pardon," he said, "I'm a bit rattled to-night. You see, I happen at this moment to be dead."

I sat down in an armchair and lit my pipe.

"What does it feel like?" I asked. I was pretty certain that I had to deal with a madman.

A smile flickered over his drawn face. "I'm not mad – yet. Say, sir, I've been watching you, and I reckon you're a cool customer. I reckon, too, you're an honest man, and not afraid of playing a bold hand. I'm going to confide in you. I need help worse than any man ever needed it, and I want to know if I can count you in."

"Get on with your yarn," I said, "and I'll tell you."

He seemed to brace himself for a great effort, and then started on the queerest rigmarole. I didn't get hold of it at first, and I had to stop and ask him questions. But here is the gist of it:

He was an American, from Kentucky, and after college,

3 **gulp:** Schluck, Zug.
5 **rattled:** nervös.
10 **to flicker:** huschen.
drawn: abgehärmt.
13 **to play a bold hand:** ein gewagtes Spiel treiben.
14 **to confide in s.o.:** sich jdm. anvertrauen, jdm. vertrauen.
15 **to count s.o. in:** mit jdm. rechnen.
16 **yarn:** (fig.) Garn, Geschichte, Erzählung.
17 **to brace o.s. for s.th.** (fig.): sich auf etwas gefaßt machen.
18 **queer:** komisch, seltsam.
rigmarole: Geschwätz, Theater, Zirkus.
20 **gist:** das Wesentliche, Kern.

being pretty well off, he had started out to see the world. He wrote a bit, and acted as war correspondent for a Chicago paper, and spent a year or two in South-Eastern Europe. I gathered that he was a fine linguist, and had got to know pretty well the society in those parts. He spoke familiarly of many names that I remembered to have seen in the newspapers.

He had played about with politics, he told me, at first for the interest of them, and then because he couldn't help himself. I read him as a sharp, restless fellow, who always wanted to get down to the roots of things. He got a little further down than he wanted.

I am giving you what he told me as well as I could make it out. Away behind all the Governments and the armies there was a big subterranean movement going on, engineered by very dangerous people. He had come on it by accident; it fascinated him; he went further, and then he got caught. I gathered that most of the people in it were the sort of educated anarchists that make revolutions, but that beside them there were financiers who were playing for money. A clever man can make big profits on a falling market, and it suited the book of both classes to set Europe by the ears.

He told me some queer things that explained a lot that had puzzled me – things that happened in the Balkan

1 **well off:** wohlhabend.
4 **linguist:** Sprachwissenschaftler(in), Sprachkundige(r).
15 **subterranean movement:** Untergrundbewegung.
16 **to engineer** (fig.): (geschickt) in die Wege leiten, organisieren.
22 **to suit the book of s.o.:** jdm. in den Kram passen.
23 **to set s.o. by the ears:** jdn. aufhetzen.
25 **to puzzle:** verwirren, irritieren.
25 f. **Balkan War:** einer der beiden Balkankriege (1912/13).

War, how one state suddenly came out on top, why alliances were made and broken, why certain men disappeared, and where the sinews of war came from. The aim of the whole conspiracy was to get Russia and Germany at loggerheads.

When I asked why, he said that the anarchist lot thought it would given them their chance. Everything would be in the melting-pot, and they looked to see a new world emerge. The capitalists would rake in the shekels, and make fortunes by buying up wreckage. Capital, he said, had no conscience and no fatherland. Besides, the Jew was behind it, and the Jew hated Russia worse than hell.

"Do you wonder?" he cried. "For three hundred years they have been persecuted, and this is the return match for the *pogroms*. The Jew is everywhere, but you have to go far down the backstairs to find him. Take any big Teutonic business concern. If you have dealings with it the first man you meet is Prince *von und zu* Something, an elegant young man who talks Eton-and-Harrow

1 f. **alliance:** Allianz, Bündnis.
3 **sinew:** Sehne.
4 **conspiracy:** Verschwörung.
4 f. **to get s.o. at loggerheads:** Streit bei jdm. bewirken.
8 **melting-pot:** Schmelztiegel.
9 **to rake in:** zusammenraffen, scheffeln.
10 **shekels** (infml.): Moneten, Geld.
wreckage: Trümmer, Wrackteile.
12 **Jew:** Jude, Jüdin.
15 **to persecute:** verfolgen.
16 **pogrom:** (Juden-)Verfolgung.
17 **backstairs** (pl.): Hintertreppe.
20 f. **Eton-and-Harrow English:** gehobenes Englisch. (In Eton und Harrow befinden sich zwei berühmte höhere Schulen Englands.)

English. But he cuts no ice. If your business is big, you get behind him and find a prognathous Westphalian with a retreating brow and the manners of a hog. He is the German business man that gives your English papers the shakes. But if you're on the biggest kind of job and are bound to get to the real boss, ten to one you are brought up against a little white-faced Jew in a bath-chair with an eye like a rattlesnake. Yes, sir, he is the man who is ruling the world just now, and he has his knife in the Empire of the Tzar, because his aunt was outraged and his father flogged in some one-horse location on the Volga."

I could not help saying that his Jew-anarchists seemed to have got left behind a little.

"Yes and no," he said. "They won up to a point, but they struck a bigger thing that money, a thing that could't be bought, the old elemental fighting instincts of man. If you're going to be killed you invent some kind of flag and country to fight for, and if you survive

1 **to cut no ice** (infml.): keinen Eindruck machen, nicht ‚ziehen'.
2 **prognathous:** mit hervorstehendem Unterkiefer.
3 **retreating:** fliehend, zurückweichend.
brow: Stirn.
hog: (Haus-)Schwein.
7 f. **a little white-faced Jew … rattlesnake:** Diese vielzitierte Textstelle repräsentiert nicht etwa Buchans eigene antisemitischen Ansichten, denn er hatte einige jüdische Freunde, sondern spielt eher auf die deutsche Kriegsmaschinerie mit ihrer aristokratischen Fassade und jüdischen Koordinator-Figuren in der Wirtschaft wie Walther Rathenau von der AEG an (*bath-chair:* Rollstuhl; *rattlesnake:* Klapperschlange).
10 **Tzar:** Zar.
11 **outraged:** vergewaltigt.
to flog: prügeln, schlagen; (infml.) verkloppen.

you get to love the thing. Those foolish devils of soldiers have found something they care for, and that has upset the pretty plan laid in Berlin and Vienna. But my friends haven't played their last card by a long sight. They've gotten the ace up their sleeves, and unless I can keep alive for a month they are going to play it and win."

"But I thought you were dead," I put in.

"*Mors janua vitae*," he smiled. (I recognized the quotation: it was about all the Latin I knew.) "I'm coming to that, but I've got to put you wise about a lot of things first. If you read your newspaper, I guess you know the name of Constantine Karolides?"

I sat up at that, for I had been reading about him that very afternoon.

"He is the man that has wrecked all their games. He is the one big brain in the whole show, and he happens also to be an honest man. Therefore he has been marked down these twelve months past. I found that out – not that it was difficult, for any fool could guess as much. But I found out the way they were going to get him, and that knowledge was deadly. That's why I have had to decease."

5 **to have got the ace up one's sleeve:** (fig.) das As (einen Trumpf) im Ärmel haben (*gotten: got*).
9 **"Mors janua vitae"** (Lat.): »Der Tod ist das Tor zum Leben«; Zitat aus der ersten Predigt von Bernhard von Clairvaux, *In Transitu St. Malachi* (um 1150).
9 f. **quotation:** Zitat.
11 **to put s.o. wise about s.th.:** jdn. über etwas aufklären.
18 f. **to be marked down:** bestimmt, vorgemerkt sein.
23 **to decease:** ableben, sterben.

He had another drink, and I mixed it for him myself, for I was getting interested in the beggar.

"They cant't get him in his own land, for he had a bodyguard of Epirots that would skin their grandmothers. But on the 15th day of June he is coming to this city. The British Foreign Office has taken to having international tea-parties, and the biggest of them is due on that date. Now Karolides is reckoned the principal guest, and if my friends have their way he will never return to his admiring countrymen."

"That's simple enough, anyhow," I said. "You can warn him and keep him at home."

"And play their game?" he asked sharply. "If he does not come they win, for he's the only man that can straighten out the tangle. And if his Government are warned he won't come, for he does not know how big the stakes will be on June the 15th."

"What about the British Government?" I said. "They're not going to let their guests be murdered. Tip them the wink, and they'll take extra precautions."

"No good. They might stuff your city with plain-clothes detectives and double the police and Constantine

2 **beggar** (infml.): Kerl, Bursche.
4 **Epirot:** Bewohner des Epirus. einer Bergregion im Nordwesten Griechenlands, von wo aus dic Gricchen gefürchtete Guerillatruppen gegen Albanien formierten.
6 **British Foreign Office:** britisches Außenministerium.
15 **tangle:** Durcheinander, Verwicklung; Auseinandersetzung, schwierige Lage.
17 **stakes:** (Spiel-)Einsätze.
19 f. **to tip s.o. a wink:** jdm. einen Tip, Hinweis geben.
21 **plain-clothes:** in Zivil.

would still be a doomed man. My friends are not playing this game for candy. They want a big occasion for the taking off, with the eyes of all Europe on it. He'll be murdered by an Austrian, and there'll be plenty of evidence to show the connivance of the big folk in Vienna and Berlin. It will all be an infernal lie, of course, but the case will look black enough to the world. I'm not talking hot air, my friend. I happen to know every detail of the hellish contrivance, and I can tell you it will be the most finished piece of blackguardism since the Borgias. But it's not going to come off it there's a certain man who knows the wheels of the business alive right here in London on the 15th day of June. And that man is going to be your servant, Franklin P. Scudder."

I was getting to like the little chap. His jaw had shut like a rat-trap, and there was the fire of battle in his gimlety eyes. If he was spinning me a yarn he could act up to it.

"Where did you find out this story?" I asked.

"I got the first hint in an inn on the Achensee in Tyrol.

1 **doomed:** (zum Tod) verurteilt; verloren.
2 **candy:** Kandiszucker (BE); Süßigkeiten (AE).
5 **connivance:** stillschweigende Duldung, bewußtes Übersehen.
8 **hot air** (infml.): leeres Geschwätz, blauer Dunst.
9 **contrivance:** Erfindung, Bewerkstelligung.
10 **blackguardism:** Schurkerei.
11 **Borgia:** römisches Adelsgeschlecht mit mehreren berühmten Vertretern. Vor allem Cesare (1475–1507) und Lucrezia B. (1480–1519) zeichneten sich durch besondere Grausamkeit und verbrecherische Handlungen aus.
15 **Scudder:** sprechender Name; wörtl.: (Dahin-)Jagender.
18 **to spin a yarn:** fabulieren, Geschichten erzählen.

That set me inquiring, and I collected my other clues in a fur-shop in the Galician quarter of Buda, in a Strangers' Club in Vienna, and in a little bookshop off the Racknitzstrasse in Leipsic. I completed my evidence ten days ago in Paris. I can't tell you the details now, for it's something of a history. When I was quite sure in my own mind I judged it my business to disappear, and I reached this city by a mighty queer circuit. I left Paris a dandified young French-American, and I sailed from Hamburg a Jew diamond merchant. In Norway I was an English student of Ibsen collecting material for lectures, but when I left Bergen I was a cinema-man with special ski films. And I came here from Leith with a lot of pulp-wood propositions in my pocket to put before the London newspapers. Till yesterday I thought I had muddied my trail some, and was feeling pretty happy. Then ..."

The recollection seemed to upset him, and he gulped down some more whisky.

1 **clue:** Hinweis, Anhaltspunkt, Fingerzeig.
2 **Galician:** galizisch, auf Galizien (Landschaft im Grenzgebiet zwischen Polen und Rußland am Nordhang der Karpaten) bezogen.
Buda: westliches Stadtgebiet von Budapest.
8 **circuit:** Kreisbogen.
9 **dandified:** dandy-, stutzerhaft.
11 **Ibsen:** Henrik I. (1828–1906), norwegischer Dramatiker.
12 **Bergen:** Hafenstadt im Südwesten Norwegens.
13 **Leith:** Hafen von Edinburgh.
14 **pulp-wood:** (importierter) Zellstoff, der zu *pulp*, einem Brei zur Papierherstellung, verarbeitet wurde.
proposition: Angebot, Geschäft.
16 **to muddy one's trail:** seine Spur verwischen.
18 **recollection:** Erinnerung.
18 f. **to gulp down:** (Getränk) hinuntergießen.

"Then I saw a man standing in the street outside this block. I used to stay close in my room all day, and only slip out after dark for an hour or two. I watched him for a bit from my window, and I thought I recognized him. . . . He came in and spoke to the porter. . . . When I came back from my walk last night I found a card in my letter-box. It bore the name of the man I want least to meet on God's earth."

I think that the look in my companion's eyes, the sheer naked scare on his face, completed my conviction of his honesty. My own voice sharpened a bit as I asked him what he did next.

"I realized that I was bottled as sure as a pickled herring, and that there was only one way out. I had to die. If my pursuers knew I was dead they would go to sleep again."

"How did you manage it?"

"I told the man that valets me that I was feeling pretty bad, and I got myself up to look like death. That wasn't difficult, for I'm no slouch at disguises. Then I got a corpse – you can always get a body in London if you know where to go for it. I fetched it back in a trunk on the top of a four-wheeler, and I had to be assisted upstairs to my room. You see I had to pile up some evidence for the inquest. I went to bed and got my man to

13 **bottled:** (fig.) eingeschlossen, gefangen.
pickled: mariniert.
15 **pursuer:** Verfolger(in).
18 **to valet s.o.:** jdn. bedienen, versorgen.
20 **slouch** (infml.): Niete, Nichtskönner(in), ‚Flasche'.
disguise: Verkleidung.
23 **four-wheeler:** Pferdewagen, -kutsche mit vier Rädern.
25 **inquest:** gerichtliche Untersuchung.

mix me a sleeping-draught, and then told him to clear out. He wanted to fetch a doctor, but I swore some and said I couldn't abide leeches. When I was left alone I started in to fake up that corpse. He was my size, and I judged had perished from too much alcohol, so I put some spirits handy about the place. The jaw was the weak point in the likeness, so I blew it away with a revolver. I daresay there will be somebody to-morrow to swear to having heard a shot, but there are no neighbours on my floor, and I guessed I could risk it. So I left the body in bed dressed up in my pyjamas, with a revolver lying on the bed-clothes and a considerable mess around. Then I got into a suit of clothes I had kept waiting for emergencies. I didn't dare to shave for fear of leaving tracks, and besides, it wasn't any kind of use my trying to get into the streets. I had had you in my mind all day, and there seemed nothing to do but to make an appeal to you. I watched from my window till I saw you come home, and then slipped down the stair to meet you. . . . There, sir, I guess you know about as much as me of this business."

He sat blinking like an owl, fluttering with nerves and yet desperately determined. By this time I was pretty well convinced that he was going straight with me. It was the wildest sort of narrative, but I had heard in my

1 **sleeping-draught:** Schlaftrunk.
3 **I couldn't abide:** ich konnte nicht ausstehen, ertragen.
leech: Blutegel; (infml.) Arzt.
4 **to fake up:** verfälschen, zurechtmachen.
22 **to blink:** blinzeln, zwinkern.
to flutter: flattern (Herz, Nerven).
24 **to go straight with s.o.:** aufrichtig zu jdm. sein.
25 **narrative:** Erzählung.

time many steep tales which had turned out to be true, and I had made a practice of judging the man rather than the story. If he had wanted to get a location in my flat, and then cut my throat, he would have pitched a milder yarn.

"Hand me your key," I said, "and I'll take a look at the corpse. Excuse my caution, but I'm bound to verify a bit if I can."

He shook his head mournfully. "I reckoned you'd ask for that, but I haven't got it. It's on my chain on the dressing-table. I had to leave it behind, for I couldn't leave any clues to breed suspicions. The gentry who are after me are pretty bright-eyed citizens. You'll have to take me on trust for the night, and to-morrow you'll get proof of the corpse business right enough."

I thought for an instant or two. "Right. I'll trust you for the night. I'll lock you into this room and keep the key. Just one word, Mr Scudder. I believe you're straight, but if so be you are not I should warn you that I'm a handy man with a gun."

"Sure", he said, jumping up with some briskness. "I haven't the privilege of your name, sir, but let me tell you that you're a white man. I'll thank you to lend me a razor."

I took him into my bedroom and turned him loose. In half an hour's time a figure came out that I scarcely rec-

4 **to pitch:** (Ton) anschlagen, -stimmen.
7 **to verify:** bestätigen, (über)prüfen, nachweisen.
9 **mournfully** (adv.): traurig.
13 **bright-eyed** (fig.): aufgeweckt, intelligent.
21 **briskness:** Schwung, Munterkeit.
25 **to turn s.o. loose:** jdn. loslassen.

ognized. Only his gimlety, hungry eyes were the same. He was shaved clean, his hair was parted in the middle, and he had cut his eyebrows. Further, he carried himself as if he had been drilled, and was the very model, even to the brown complexion, of some British officers who had had a long spell in India. He had a monocle, too, which he stuck in his eye, and every trace of the American had gone out of his speech.

"My hat! Mr Scudder –" I stammered.

"Not Mr Scudder," he corrected; "Captain Theophilus Digby, of the 40th Gurkhas, presently home on leave. I'll thank you to remember that, sir."

I made him up a bed in my smoking-room and sought my own couch, more cheerful than I had been for the past month. Things did happen occasionally, even in this God-forgotten metropolis.

I woke next morning to hear my man, Paddock, making the deuce of a row at the smoking-room door. Paddock was a fellow I had done a good turn to out on the Selakwi, and I had inspanned him as my servant as soon as I got to England. He had about as much gift of the

5 **complexion:** Gesichtsfarbe, Teint.
6 **spell:** Weile, Zeit.
9 **to stammer:** stammeln, stottern.
11 **Gurkha:** Angehöriger eines indischen Volkes in der britischen Armee.
17 **Paddock:** sprechender Name; wörtl.: (Pferde-)Koppel; (Scot.) Frosch, Kröte.
18 **deuce** (infml.): *devil.*
19 f. **Selakwi:** Selukwe, Stadt in Rhodesien (Simbabwe).
20 **to inspan** (S. Afr.): einspannen.
21 f. **to have the gift of the gab:** ein flottes Mundwerk haben.

gab as a hippopotamus, and was not a great hand at valeting, but I knew I could count on his loyalty.

"Stop that row, Paddock," I said. "There's a friend of mine, Captain – Captain" (I couldn't remember the name) "dossing down in there. Get breakfast for two and then come and speak to me."

I told Paddock a fine story about how my friend was a great swell, with his nerves pretty bad from overwork, who wanted absolute rest and stillness. Nobody had got to know he was here, or he would be besieged by communications from the India Office and the Prime Minister and his cure would be ruined. I am bound to say Scudder played up splendidly when he came to breakfast. He fixed Paddock with his eyeglass, just like a British officer, asked him about the Boer War, and slung out at me a lot of stuff about imaginary pals. Paddock couldn't learn to call me "sir", but he "sirred" Scudder as if his life depended on it.

I left him with the newspaper and a box of cigars, and went down to the City till luncheon. When I got back the lift-man had an important face.

1 **hippopotamus:** Nil-, Flußpferd.
5 **to doss:** pennen.
8 **swell** (infml.): hohes Tier, Mordskerl.
10 **to besiege:** belagern; (fig.) bestürmen, bedrängen.
11 **India Office:** Reichsamt für die (ehemalige) britische Kronkolonie Indien.
15 **Boer War:** Burenkrieg (1899–1902) zwischen England und den Burenstaaten Transvaal und Oranjefreistaat (Republik Südafrika), aus dem England siegreich hervorging.
16 **to sling s.th. out at s.o.** (infml.): jdm. etwas vorsetzen.
20 **luncheon:** Mittagessen; Imbiß.

"Nawsty business 'ere this morning, sir. Gent in No. 15 been and shot 'isself. They've just took 'im to the mortiary. The police are up there now."

I ascended to No. 15, and found a couple of bobbies and an inspector busy making an examination. I asked a few idiotic questions, and they soon kicked me out. Then I found the man that had valeted Scudder, and pumped him, but I could see he suspected nothing. He was a whining fellow with a churchyard face, and half-a-crown went far to console him.

I attended the inquest next day. A partner of some publishing firm gave evidence that the deceased had brought him wood-pulp propositions, and had been, he believed, an agent of an American business. The jury found it a case of suicide while of unsound mind, and the few effects were handed over to the American Consul to deal with. I gave Scudder a full account of the affair, and it interested him greatly. He said he wished he could have attended the inquest, for he reckoned it would be about as spicy as to read one's own obituary notice.

1 **nawsty:** *nasty.*
gent (infml.): Herr.
2 **'isself:** *himself.*
2 f. **mortiary:** Leichenschauhaus.
4 **to ascend:** hinaufgehen.
8 **to pump s.o.:** jdn. ausfragen, -horchen, -holen.
9 **to whine:** quengeln, jammern.
churchyard: Friedhof.
10 **to console s.o.:** jdn. trösten.
20 **spicy:** (fig.) würzig, pikant, witzig.
20 f. **obituary notice:** Todesanzeige, Nachruf.

The first two days he stayed with me in that back room he was very peaceful. He read and smoked a bit, and made a heap of jottings in a note-book, and every night we had a game of chess, at which he beat me hollow. I think he was nursing his nerves back to health, for he had had a pretty trying time. But on the third day I could see he was beginning to get restless. He fixed up a list of the days till June 15th, and ticked each off with a red pencil, making remarks in shorthand against them. I would find him sunk in a brown study, with his sharp eyes abstracted, and after those spells of meditation he was apt to be very despondent.

Then I could see that he began to get edgy again. He listened for little noises, and was always asking me if Paddock could be trusted. Once or twice he got very peevish, and apologized for it. I didn't blame him. I made every allowance, for he had taken on a fairly stiff job.

It was not the safety of his own skin that troubled him, but the success of the scheme he had planned. That little man was clean grit all through, without a soft spot in him. One night he was very solemn.

3 **jotting:** (kurze) Notiz.
4 **to beat s.o. hollow** (infml.): jdn. haushoch besiegen.
11 **abstracted:** geistesabwesend.
12 **to be apt to be s.th.:** dazu neigen, etwas zu sein, üblicherweise etwas sein.
despondent: verzagt, mutlos.
13 **edgy:** (fig.) bissig, reizbar, gereizt.
16 **peevish:** mißgelaunt.
17 **stiff** (fig.): hart (Kampf); schwierig (Aufgabe).
21 **grit** (fig.): Mut, Schneid, Entschlossenheit.
22 **solemn:** feierlich.

"Say, Hannay," he said, "I judge I should let you a bit deeper into this business. I should hate to go out without leaving somebody else to put up a fight." And he began to tell me in detail what I had only heard from him vaguely.

I did not give him very close attention. The fact is, I was more interested in his own adventures than in his high politics. I reckoned that Karolides and his affairs were not my business, leaving all that to him. So a lot that he said slipped clean out of my memory. I remember that he was very clear that the danger to Karolides would not begin till he had got to London, and would come from the very highest quarters, where there would be no thought of suspicion. He mentioned the name of a woman – Julia Czechenyi – as having something to do with the danger. She would be the decoy, I gathered, to get Karolides out of the care of his guards. He talked, too, about a Black Stone and a man that lisped in his speech, and he described very particularly somebody that he never referred to without a shudder – an old man with a young voice who could hood his eyes like a hawk.

He spoke a good deal about death, too. He was mortally anxious about winning through with his job, but he didn't care a rush for his life.

"I reckon it's like going to sleep when you are pretty

16 **decoy:** (Fig.) Köder, Lockvogel.

19 **to lisp:** lispeln.

21 **to hood:** eigtl.: mit einer Haube, Kappe bedecken; hier: (ver)schließen.

22 **hawk:** Falke; Habicht.

25 **not to care a rush for s.th.:** sich keinen Deut um etwas scheren.

well tired out, and waking to find a summer day with the scent of hay coming in at the window. I used to thank God for such mornings way back in the Blue-Grass country, and I guess I'll thank Him when I wake up on the other side of Jordan."

Next day he was much more cheerful, and read the life of Stonewall Jackson much of the time. I went out to dinner with a mining engineer I had got to see on business, and came back about half-past ten in time for our game of chess before turning in.

I had a cigar in my mouth, I remember, as I pushed open the smoking-room door. The lights were not lit, which struck me as odd. I wondered if Scudder had turned in already.

I snapped the switch, but there was nobody there. Then I saw something in the far corner which made me drop my cigar and fall into a cold sweat.

My guest was lying sprawled on his back. There was a long knife through his heart which skewered him to the floor.

3 f. **Blue-Grass country:** Kentucky im Südosten der USA.

7 **Stonewall Jackson:** Thomas Jonathan St. J. (1824–63), General der Konföderierten im nordamerikanischen Bürgerkrieg (1861–65); von presbyterianischer Abstammung aus der Provinz Ulster (Irland).

8 **mining engineer:** Bergbauingenieur.

10 **to turn in** (infml.): in die Falle, schlafen gehen.

18 **sprawled:** ausgestreckt (daliegend).

19 **to skewer:** (auf)spießen.

Chapter II

The Milkman Sets Out on his Travels

I sat down in an armchair and felt very sick. That lasted for maybe five minutes, and was succeeded by a fit of the horrors. The poor staring white face on the floor was more than I could bear, and I managed to get a table-cloth and cover it. Then I staggered to a cupboard, found the brandy and swallowed several mouthfuls. I had seen men die violently before; indeed I had killed a few myself in the Matabele War; but this cold-blooded indoor business was different. Still I managed to pull myself together. I looked at my watch, and saw that it was half-past ten.

An idea seized me, and I went over the flat with a small-tooth comb. There was nobody there, nor any trace of anybody, but I shuttered and bolted all the windows and put the chain on the door.

By this time my wits were coming back to me, and I could think again. It took me about an hour to figure the thing out, and I did not hurry, for, unless the mur-

4 **fit:** Anfall.
7 **to stagger:** (sch)wanken, taumeln, torkeln.
10 **Matabele War:** gemeint ist vermutl. der zweite Matabele-Krieg (1896–99) in Rhodesien (Simbabwe), der von Cecil Rhodes (1853 bis 1902) und seiner British South Africa Company gegen den Matabele-Häuptling Lobengula geführt wurde.
15 **small-tooth comb:** Staubkamm.
16 **to shutter:** die Fensterläden, Rolläden schließen.
to bolt: verriegeln.
18 **wits** (pl.): Verstand, klarer Kopf.

derer came back, I had till about six o'clock in the morning for my cogitations.

I was in the soup – that was pretty clear. Any shadow of a doubt I might have had about the truth of Scudder's tale was now gone. The proof of it was lying under the table-cloth. The men who knew that he knew what he knew had found him, and had taken the best way to make certain of his silence. Yes; but he had been in my rooms four days, and his enemies must have reckoned that he had confided in me. So I would be the next to go. It might be that very night, or next day, or the day after, but my number was up all right.

Then suddenly I thought of another probability. Supposing I went out now and called in the police, or went to bed and let Paddock find the body and call them in the morning. What kind of a story was I to tell about Scudder? I had lied to Paddock about him, and the whole thing looked desperately fishy. If I made a clean breast of it and told the police everything he had told me, they would simply laugh at me. The odds were a thousand to one that I would be charged with the murder, and the circumstantial evidence was strong enough to hang me. Few people knew me in England; I had no real pal who could come forward and swear to my char-

2 **cogitation:** (Nach-)Denken, Überlegung, Gedanke(n).
3 **to be in the soup** (infml.): in der Tinte sitzen.
12 **my number is up** (infml.): meine Stunde hat geschlagen, jetzt bin ich dran.
18 **fishy** (slang): verdächtig, anrüchig, faul.
18 f. **to make a clean breast of s.th.:** etwas offen gestehen.
20 **odds:** Aussichten, Chancen.
22 **circumstantial evidence:** Indizienbeweise.
24 **to swear to s.th.:** einen Eid auf etwas ablegen.

acter. Perhaps that was what those secret enemies were playing for. They were clever enough for anything, and an English prison was as good a way of getting rid of me till after June 15th as a knife in my chest. Besides, if I told the whole story, and by any miracle was believed, I would be playing their game. Karolides would stay at home, which was what they wanted. Somehow or other the sight of Scudder's dead face had made me a passionate believer in his scheme. He was gone, but he had taken me into his confidence, and I was pretty well bound to carry on his work.

You may think this ridiculous for a man in danger of his life, but that was the way I looked at it. I am an ordinary sort of fellow, not braver than other people, but I hate to see a good man downed, and that long knife would not be the end of Scudder if I could play the game in his place.

It took me an hour or two to think this out, and by that time I had come to a decision. I must vanish somehow, and keep vanished till the end of the second week in June. Then I must somehow find a way to get in touch with the Government people and tell them what Scudder had told me. I wished to heaven he had told me more, and that I had listened more carefully to the little he had told me. I knew nothing but the barest facts. There was a big risk that, even if I weathered the other dangers, I would not be believed in the end. I must take my chance of that, and hope that something might hap-

15 **to down:** ruinieren, fertigmachen.
26 **to weather s.th.:** etwas überstehen.

pen which would confirm my tale in the eyes of the Government.

My first job was to keep going for the next three weeks. It was now the 24th day of May, and that meant twenty days of hiding before I could venture to approach the powers that be. I reckoned that two sets of people would be looking for me – Scudder's enemies to put me out of existence, and the police, who would want me for Scudder's murder. It was going to be a giddy hunt, and it was queer how the prospect comforted me. I had been slack so long that almost any chance of activity was welcome. When I had to sit alone with that corpse and wait on Fortune I was no better than a crushed worm, but if my neck's safety was to hang on my own wits I was prepared to be cheerful about it.

My next thought was whether Scudder had any papers about him to give me a better clue to the business. I drew back the table-cloth and searched his pockets, for I had no shrinking from the body. The face was wonderfully calm for a man who had been struck down in a moment. There was nothing in the breast-pocket, and only a few loose coins and a cigar-holder in the waistcoat. The trousers held a little penknife and some silver, and the side pocket of his jacket contained an old crocodile-skin cigar-case. There was no sign of the little black book in which I had seen him

1 **to confirm:** bestätigen.
5 **to venture:** (es) wagen.
9 **giddy:** schwindelerregend, wirbelnd, verrückt, wild.
11 **slack:** nachlässig.
19 **shrinking:** Scheu.
23 **waistcoat:** (Anzug-)Weste.

making notes. That had no doubt been taken by his murderer.

But as I looked up from my task I saw that some drawers had been pulled out in the writing-table. Scudder would never have left them in that state, for he was the tidiest of mortals. Someone must have been searching for something – perhaps for the pocket-book.

I went round the flat and found that everything had been ransacked – the inside of books, drawers, cupboards, boxes, even the pockets of the clothes in my wardrobe, and the sideboard in the dining-room. There was no trace of the book. Most likely the enemy had found it, but they had not found it on Scudder's body.

Then I got out an atlas and looked at a big map of the British Isles. My notion was to get off to some wild district, where my veldcraft would be of some use to me, for I would be like a trapped rat in a city. I considered that Scotland would be best, for my people were Scotch and I could pass anywhere as an ordinary Scotsman. I had half an idea at first to be a German tourist, for my father had had German partners, and I had been brought up to speak the tongue pretty fluently, not to mention having put in three years prospecting for copper in German Damaraland. But I calculated that it would be less

6 **mortal:** Sterbliche(r).
7 **pocket-book:** Notizbuch.
9 **to ransack:** durchwühlen, -stöbern, plündern, ausrauben.
15 **notion:** Gedanke, Idee, Vorstellung.
16 **veldcraft** (S.Afr.): (Überlebens-)Erfahrung im Gras- und Buschland.
23 **to prospect for s.th.:** nach etwas suchen, schürfen.
23 f. **German Damaraland:** Gebiet in Deutsch-Südwestafrika (Namibia); etwa 150 km entfernt von der Walfisch-Bai, Schauplatz des grausamen Owambo-Krieges (1904).

conspicuous to be a Scot, and less in a line with what the police might know of my past. I fixed on Galloway as the best place to go to. It was the nearest wild part of Scotland, so far as I could figure it out, and from the look of the map was not over thick with population.

A search in Bradshaw informed me that a train left St Pancras at 7.10, which would land me at any Galloway station in the late afternoon. That was well enough, but a more important matter was how I was to make my way to St Pancras, for I was pretty certain that Scudder's friends would be watching outside. This puzzled me for a bit; then I had an inspiration, on which I went to bed and slept for two troubled hours.

I got up at four and opened my bedroom shutters. The faint light of a fine summer morning was flooding the skies, and the sparrows had begun to chatter. I had a great revulsion of feeling, and felt a God-forgotten fool. My inclination was to let things slide, and trust to the British police taking a reasonable view of my case. But as I reviewed the situation I could find no arguments to bring against my decision of the previous night, so with a wry mouth I resolved to go on with my plan. I was not

1 **conspicuous:** auffallend.

2 **Galloway:** *Dumfries and Galloway:* Grafschaft im Südwesten Schottlands.

6 **Bradshaw:** (Eisenbahn-)Fahrplan, Kursbuch.

7 **St Pancras:** Londoner Endstation der Midland-Eisenbahn. Richard Hannays Reise nach Norden führt über Derby, Sheffield, Leeds und die malerische Strecke Settle–Carlisle.

14 **shutter:** Fensterladen, Rolladen.

17 **revulsion:** Umschwung, heftige Reaktion.

22 **wry:** schief, verzerrt, verzogen.
to resolve: beschließen.

feeling in any particular funk; only disinclined to go looking for trouble, if you understand me.

I hunted out a well-used tweed suit, a pair of strong nailed boots, and a flannel shirt with a collar. Into my pockets I stuffed a spare shirt, a cloth cap, some handkerchiefs, and a tooth-brush. I had drawn a good sum in gold from the bank two days before, in case Scudder should want money, and I took fifty pounds of it in sovereigns in a belt which I had brought back from Rhodesia. That was about all I wanted. Then I had a bath, and cut my moustache, which was long and drooping, into a short stubbly fringe.

Now came the next step. Paddock used to arrive punctually at 7.30 and let himself in with a latch-key. But about twenty minutes to seven, as I knew from bitter experience, the milkman turned up with a great clatter of cans, and deposited my share outside my door. I had seen that milkman sometimes when I had gone out for an early ride. He was a young man about my own height, with an ill-nourished moustache, and he wore a white overall. On him I staked all my chances.

1 **funk** (slang): Bammel, Angst.
disinclined: abgeneigt.
3 **to hunt out:** aufstöbern.
4 **flannel:** Flanell.
8 f. **sovereign:** ehemalige britische Goldmünze im Wert von 20 Schilling.
11 **moustache:** Schnurrbart.
drooping: (schlaff) herabhängend.
12 **stubbly:** stoppelig.
fringe: Franse(n), Umrandung.
14 **latch-key:** Hausschlüssel.
16 **clatter:** Klappern, Krach, Lärm.
20 **ill-nourished:** schlecht gepflegt.
21 **to stake s.th. on s.o.:** etwas auf jdn. setzen.

I went into the darkened smoking-room where the rays of morning light were beginning to creep through the shutters. There I breakfasted off a whisky-and-soda and some biscuits from the cupboard. By this time it was getting on for six o'clock. I put a pipe in my pocket and filled my pouch from the tobacco jar on the table by the fireplace.

As I poked into the tobacco my fingers touched something hard, and I drew out Scudder's little black pocket-book. . . .

That seemed to be a good omen. I lifted the cloth from the body and was amazed at the peace and dignity of the dead face. "Good-bye, old chap," I said; "I am going to do my best for you. Wish me well, wherever you are."

Then I hung about in the hall waiting for the milkman. That was the worst part of the business, for I was fairly choking to get out of doors. Six-thirty passed, then six-forty, but still he did not come. The fool had chosen this day of all days to be late.

At one minute after the quarter to seven I heard the rattle of the cans outside. I opened the front door, and there was my man, singling out my cans from a bunch he carried and whistling through his teeth. He jumped a bit at the sight of me.

"Come in here a moment," I said. "I want a word with you." And I led him to the dining-room.

6 **pouch:** Tabaksbeutel.
8 **to poke into s.th.:** in etwas (herum)stochern.
17 f. **to be choking to do s.th.** (slang): darauf brennen, etwas zu tun.
22 **rattle:** Klappern, Klirren.
23 **to single out:** aussuchen, -wählen, herausheben.

"I reckon you're a bit of a sportsman," I said, "and I want you to do me a service. Lend me your cap and overall for ten minutes, and here's a sovereign for you."

His eyes opened at the sight of the gold, and he grinned broadly. "Wot's the gyme?" he asked.

"A bet," I said. "I haven't time to explain, but to win it I've got to be a milkman for the next ten minutes. All you've got to do is to stay here till I come back. You'll be a bit late, but nobody will complain, and you'll have that quid for yourself."

"Right-o!" he said cheerily. "I ain't the man to spoil a bit of sport. 'Ere's the rig, guv'nor."

I stuck on his flat blue hat and his white overall, picked up the cans, banged my door, and went whistling downstairs. The porter at the foot told me to shut my jaw, which sounded as if my make-up was adequate.

At first I thought there was nobody in the street. Then I caught sight of a policeman a hundred yards down, and a loafer shuffling past on the other side. Some impulse made me raise my eyes to the house opposite,

6 **Wot's the gyme?:** *What is the game?*
11 **quid** (slang): Pfund Sterling.
12 **right-o** (infml.): okay, alles klar.
I ain't: *I am not.*
13 **rig:** Ausrüstung, Montur, Aufmachung (Kleidung).
guv'nor (dial.): *governor:* mein Herr, Chef (Anrede durch Untergebene).
15 **to bang:** zuschlagen, -knallen.
16 **to shut one's jaw** (infml.): den Mund halten.
17 **make-up:** Aufmachung, Maskierung.
20 **loafer:** Bummler(in), Müßiggänger(in), Faulenzer(in).
to shuffle past: vorbeischlurfen.

and there at a first-floor window was a face. As the loafer passed he looked up, and I fancied a signal was exchanged.

I crossed the street, whistling gaily and imitating the jaunty swing of the milkman. Then I took the first side street, and went up a left-hand turning which led past a bit of vacant ground. There was no one in the little street, so I dropped the milk-cans inside the hoarding and sent the hat and overall after them. I had only just put on my cloth cap when a postman came round the corner. I gave him good morning and he answered me unsuspiciously. At the moment the clock of a neighbouring church struck the hour of seven.

There was not a second to spare. As soon as I got to Euston Road I took to my heels and ran. The clock at Euston Station showed five minutes past the hour. At St Pancras I had no time to take a ticket, let alone that I had not settled upon my destination. A porter told me the platform and as I entered it I saw the train already in motion. Two station officials blocked the way, but I dodged them and clambered into the last carriage.

Three minutes later, as we were roaring through the northern tunnels, an irate guard interviewed me. He

5 **jaunty:** flott, munter, unbeschwert.
8 **hoarding:** Bau-, Bretterzaun.
15 **Euston Road:** Straße im Norden Londons.
to take to one's heels: Fersengeld geben, die Beine in die Hand nehmen.
16 **Euston Station:** Londoner Nordbahnhof.
21 **to dodge:** ausweichen, entkommen; umgehen, irreführen.
to clamber: (mühsam) klettern.
23 **irate:** zornig, wütend.

wrote out for me a ticket to Newton-Stewart, a name which had suddenly come back to my memory, and he conducted me from the first-class compartment where I had ensconced myself to a third-class smoker, occupied by a sailor and a stout woman with a child. He went off grumbling, and as I mopped my brow I observed to my companions in my broadest Scots that it was a sore job catching trains. I had already entered upon my part.

"The impidence o' that gyaird!" said the lady bitterly. "He needit a Scotch tongue to pit him in his place. He was complainin' o' this wean no haein' a ticket and her no fower till August twalmonth, and he was objectin' to this gentleman spittin'."

The sailor morosely agreed, and I started my new life in an atmosphere of protest against authority. I reminded myself that a week ago I had been finding the world dull.

1 **Newton-Stewart:** Ort in Galloway.
4 **to ensconce o.s.:** sich verstecken, sich niederlassen, es sich bequem machen.
5 **stout:** stämmig, dick, korpulent.
6 **to grumble:** murren.
to mop one's brow: sich das Gesicht abwischen.
7 **sore:** schlimm, heikel.
9 **impidence:** *impudence.*
gyaird: *guard.*
10 **needit:** *needed.*
to pit s.o. in his, her place: jdn. (scharf) auf seinen Platz verweisen; (fig.) jdn. zurechtweisen (*pit* [Scot.]: *put*).
11 **wean** (Scot.): Kleinkind, Kleine(r, -s).
haein': *having.*
12 **fower:** *four.*
twalmonth: *twelvemonth.*
14 **morosely** (adv.): mürrisch, verdrießlich.

Chapter III

The Adventure of the Literary Innkeeper

I had a solemn time travelling north that day. It was fine May weather, with the hawthorn flowering on every hedge, and I asked myself why, when I was still a free man, I had stayed on in London and not got the good of this heavenly country. I didn't dare face the restaurant car, but I got a luncheon-basket at Leeds and shared it with the fat woman. Also I got the morning's papers, with news about starters for the Derby and the beginning of the cricket season, and some paragraphs about how Balkan affairs were settling down and a British squadron was going to Kiel.

When I had done with them I got out Scudder's little black pocket-book and studied it. It was pretty well filled with jottings, chiefly figures, though now and then a name was printed in. For example, I found the words "Hofgaard", "Luneville" and "Avocado" pretty often, and especially the word "Pavia".

Now I was certain that Scudder never did anything

4 **hawthorn:** Weißdorn.

10 **starter:** Pferd am Start, Rennteilnehmer(in).

12 f. **a British squadron was going to Kiel:** 1914 besuchte ein britisches Flottengeschwader Kiel zur Demonstration der augenscheinlich guten Beziehungen zwischen Großbritannien und Deutschland. Aber bald darauf wurde die Flotte (auf Testbasis) mobil gemacht (*squadron:* Geschwader).

18 f. **Hofgaard / Luneville / Avocado / Pavia:** vermutl. Namen für einen echten Geheimcode (vgl. Nachwort). *Pavia* bezieht sich viell. auch auf den befürchteten Angriff der Deutschen auf die britische Flotte.

without a reason, and I was pretty sure that there was a cypher in all this. That is a subject which has always interested me, and I did a bit at it myself once as intelligence-officer at Delagoa Bay during the Boer War. I have a head for things like chess and puzzles, and I used to reckon myself pretty good at finding out cyphers. This one looked like the numerical kind where sets of figures correspond to the letters of the alphabet, but any fairly shrewd man can find the clue to that sort after an hour or two's work, and I didn't think Scudder would have been content with anything so easy. So I fastened on the printed words, for you can make a pretty good numerical cypher if you have a key word which gives you the sequence of the letters.

I tried for hours, but none of the words answered. Then I fell asleep and woke at Dumfries just in time to bundle out and get into the slow Galloway train. There was a man on the platform whose looks I didn't like, but he never glanced at me, and when I caught sight of myself in the mirror of an automatic machine I didn't wonder. With my brown face, my old tweeds, and my slouch, I was the very model of one of the hill farmers who were crowding into the third-class carriages.

2 **cypher:** Chiffre, Geheimschrift; (fig.) Schlüssel, Kennwort.
3 f. **intelligence-officer:** Nachrichtenoffizier.
4 **Delagoa Bay:** Die Hafenstadt Lourenço Marques an der Delagoa-Bai in Portugiesisch-Ostafrika (Moçambique) war ein bedeutendes Zentrum zur Versorgung der Buren-Republiken mit Kriegsmaterial per Eisenbahn.
9 **shrewd:** schlau, klug, scharfsinnig.
16 f. **to bundle out:** sich davonmachen, aussteigen.
21 **slouch:** krumme, nachlässige Haltung; herabhängende Hutkrempe.

I travelled with half a dozen in an atmosphere of shag and clay pipes. They had come from the weekly market, and their mouths were full of prices. I heard accounts of how the lambing had gone up the Cairn and the Deuch and a dozen other mysterious waters. Above half the men had lunched heavily and were highly flavoured with whisky, but they took no notice of me. We rumbled slowly into a land of little wooded glens and then to a great wide moorland place, gleaming with lochs, with high hills showing northwards.
About five o'clock the carriage had emptied, and I was left alone as I had hoped. I got out at the next station, a little place whose name I scarcely noted, set right in the heart of a bog. It reminded me of one of those forgotten little stations in thc Karroo. An old station-master was digging in his garden, and with his spade over his shoulder sauntered to the train, took charge of a parcel, and went back to his potatoes. A child of ten re-

1 **shag:** Tabaksorte.
2 **clay:** Ton-, Keramik-.
4 **Cairn:** Cairn Water; fließt von Moniaive aus bei Dumfries in den Fluß Nith.
5 **Deuch:** Deugh, Nebenfluß des Ken, den Hannay mit dem Zug bei Parton in Galloway überquert; Schauplatz der Episode mit dem literarischen Schankwirt.
8 **to rumble:** rumpeln.
glen (Scot., Ir.): Bergschlucht, Klamm.
9 **to gleam:** schimmern, leuchten.
10 **loch** (Scot.): See.
14 **bog:** Sumpf, Moor.
15 **Karroo:** Karree-Berge, Höhenzug in Kapland (Republik Südafrika).
17 **to saunter:** schlendern.

ceived my ticket, and I emerged on a white road that straggled over the brown moor.

It was a gorgeous spring evening, with every hill showing as clear as a cut amethyst. The air had the queer, rooty smell of bogs, but it was as fresh as mid-ocean, and it had the strangest effect on my spirits. I actually felt light-hearted. I might have been a boy out for a spring holiday tramp, instead of a man of thirty-seven very much wanted by the police. I felt just as I used to feel when I was starting for a big trek on a frosty morning on the high veld. If you believe me, I swung along that road whistling. There was no plan of campaign in my head, only just to go on and on in this blessed, honest-smelling hill country, for every mile put me in better humour with myself.

In a roadside planting I cut a walking-stick of hazel, and presently struck off the highway up a bypath which followed the glen of a brawling stream. I reckoned that I was still far ahead of any pursuit, and for that night might please myself. It was some hours since I had tasted food, and I was getting very hungry when I came to a herd's cottage set in a nook beside a waterfall. A

2 **to straggle:** sich mit vielen Windungen hinziehen, kreuz und quer verlaufen.

3 **gorgeous:** prächtig, wunderbar.

10 **trek** (S. Afr.): Trekking-Tour, (anstrengender) Marsch.

16 **hazel:** Haselnußstrauch, -zweig.

17 **to strike off s.th.:** von etwas abbiegen.
bypath: Seitenweg.

18 **brawling:** rauschend (Fluß).

22 **herd:** Hirt(in).
nook: Winkel, Ecke, stilles Plätzchen.

brown-faced woman was standing by the door, and greeted me with the kindly shyness of moorland places. When I asked for a night's lodging she said I was welcome to the "bed in the loft", and very soon she set before me a hearty meal of ham and eggs, scones, and thick sweet milk.

At the darkening her man came in from the hills, a lean giant, who in one step covered as much ground as three paces of ordinary mortals. They asked no questions, for they had the perfect breeding of all dwellers in the wilds, but I could see they set me down as a kind of dealer, and I took some trouble to confirm their view. I spoke a lot about cattle, of which my host knew little, and I picked up from him a good deal about the local Galloway markets, which I tucked away in my memory for future use. At ten I was nodding in my chair, and the "bed in the loft" received a weary man who never opened his eyes till five o'clock set the little homestead a-going once more.

They refused any payment, and by six I had breakfasted and was striding southwards again. My notion was to return to the railway line a station or two farther

3 **lodging:** Wohnung, Unterkunft, Quartier.
4 **loft:** Dach-, Heuboden, Speicher.
5 **scone:** kleiner runder weicher (Tee-)Kuchen, mit Butter serviert.
10 **breeding:** Erziehung, Benehmen, (gute) Lebensart.
dweller: Bewohner(in).
11 **to set s.o. down as s.th.:** jdn. für etwas halten.
15 **to tuck away:** wegstecken.
16 **to nod:** (ein)nicken, (sitzend) schlafen.
18 **homestead:** Heimstätte.
19 **a-going:** *going.*
21 **to stride:** schreiten, gehen.

on than the place where I had alighted yesterday and to double back. I reckoned that that was the safest way, for the police would naturally assume that I was always making farther from London in the direction of some western port. I thought I had still a good bit of a start, for, as I reasoned, it would take some hours to fix the blame on me, and several more to identify the fellow who got on board the train at St Pancras.

It was the same jolly, clear spring weather, and I simply could not contrive to feel careworn. Indeed I was in better spirits than I had been for months. Over a long ridge of moorland I took my road, skirting the side of a high hill which the herd had called Cairnsmore of Fleet. Nesting curlews and plovers were crying everywhere, and the links of green pasture by the streams were dotted with young lambs. All the slackness of the past months was slipping from my bones, and I stepped out like a four-year-old. By-and-by I came to a swell of

1 **to alight:** aussteigen.
2 **to double back:** kehrtmachen, zurücklaufen.
9 **jolly:** angenehm, herrlich (Wetter).
10 **to contrive to do s.th.:** es fertigbringen, etwas zu tun.
careworn: von Sorgen erfüllt, gramerfüllt.
12 **ridge:** (Gebirgs-)Grat, Kamm; Berg-, Hügelkette.
to skirt: entlanggehen.
13 f. **Cairnsmore of Fleet:** Berg in Galloway.
14 **curlew:** Brachvogel.
plover: Regenpfeifer, Kiebitz.
15 **pasture:** Weideland.
16 **dotted:** gesprenkelt, übersät.
slackness: Trägheit.
18 **by-and-by:** nach einer Weile.
swell: kleine Anhöhe, sanfte Steigung.

moorland which dipped to the vale of a little river, and a mile away in the heather I saw the smoke of a train. The station, when I reached it, proved to be ideal for my purpose. The moor surged up around it and left room only for the single line, the slender siding, a waiting-room, an office, the station-master's cottage, and a tiny yard of gooseberries and sweet-william. There seemed no road to it from anywhere, and to increase the desolation the waves of a tarn lapped on their grey granite beach half a mile away. I waited in the deep heather till I saw the smoke of an east-going train on the horizon. Then I approached the tiny booking-office and took a ticket for Dumfries.

The only occupants of the carriage were an old shepherd and his dog – a wall-eyed brute that I mistrusted. The man was asleep, and on the cushions beside him was that morning's *Scotsman*. Eagerly I seized on it, for I fancied it would tell me something.

There were two columns about the Portland Place Mur-

1 **to dip:** sich neigen, abfallen.
vale (poet.): Tal.
2 **heather:** Heidekraut, Erika.
4 **to surge up:** ansteigen.
5 **siding:** Neben-, Rangiergleis.
7 **gooseberry:** Stachelbeere.
sweet-william: Bartnelke (Gartenpflanze).
9 **desolation:** Verlassenheit, Einsamkeit, Trostlosigkeit.
tarn: kleiner Bergsee.
to lap: plätschern.
15 **wall-eyed:** glasäugig (Tiere).
brute: (unvernünftiges) Tier; (fig.) Untier, Scheusal.
17 **"Scotsman":** 1826 gegründete renommierte Tageszeitung Edinburghs.

der, as it was called. My man Paddock had given the alarm and had the milkman arrested. Poor devil, it looked as if the latter had earned his sovereign hardly; but for me he had been cheap at the price, for he seemed to have occupied the police the better part of the day. In the latest news I found a further instalment of the story. The milkman had been released, I read, and the true criminal, about whose identity the police were reticent, was believed to have got away from London by one of the northern lines. There was a short note about me as the owner of the flat. I guessed the police had stuck that in, as a clumsy contrivance to persuade me that I was unsuspected.

There was nothing else in the paper, nothing about foreign politics or Karolides, or the things that had interested Scudder. I laid it down, and found that we were approaching the station at which I had got out yesterday. The potato-digging station-master had been gingered up into some activity, for the west-going train was waiting to let us pass, and from it had descended three men who were asking him questions. I supposed that they were the local police, who had been stirred up by Scotland Yard, and had traced me as far as this one-horse siding. Sitting well back in the shadow I watched them carefully. One of them had a book, and took down notes. The old potato-digger seemed to have turned peevish, but the child who had collected my

6 **instalment:** Fortsetzung (Roman).
9 **to be reticent about s.th.:** in bezug auf etwas zurückhaltend, verschwiegen sein.
12 **clumsy:** unbeholfen, ungeschickt, plump.
18 f. **to ginger s.o. up into s.th.:** jdn. zu etwas anfeuern.

ticket was talking volubly. All the party looked out across the moor where the white road departed. I hoped they were going to take up my tracks there.

As we moved away from that station my companion woke up. He fixed me with a wandering glance, kicked his dog viciously, and inquired where he was. Clearly he was very drunk.

"That's what comes o' bein' a teetotaller," he observed in bitter regret.

I expressed my surprise that in him I should have met a blue-ribbon stalwart.

"Ay, but I'm a strong teetotaller," he said pugnaciously. "I took the pledge last Martinmas, and I havena touched a drop o' whisky sinsyne. No even at Hogmanay, though I was sair temptit."

1 **volubly** (adv.): redegewandt, redselig, wortreich.
6 **viciously** (adv.): bösartig, boshaft, gemein.
8 **o':** *of.*
teetotaller: Abstinenzler(in), Antialkoholiker(in).
11 **blue-ribbon:** blaues Band, Hosenbandorden, Abzeichen einer Abstinenzler-Vereinigung; Zeichen der Abstinenz.
stalwart: strammer Kerl, treuer Anhänger, Unentwegter.
12 **ay** (auch: *aye*) (Scot.): ja.
pugnaciously (adv.): kampflustig, kämpferisch, streitsüchtig; mit großem Einsatz, vehement.
13 **to take the pledge:** dem Alkohol abschwören.
Martinmas: Feiertag des hl. Martin, Schutzpatrons der bekehrten Alkoholiker, am 11. November; in Schottland auch einer von vier Zahltagen im Jahr, an dem ein Jahrmarkt abgehalten und viel getrunken wurde.
14 **sinsyne** (Scot.): *since then.*
14 f. **Hogmanay** (Scot.): Silvester.
15 **sair:** *sore* (adv., dial.): stark, sehr.
to tempt s.o.: jdn. reizen, in Versuchung führen, herausfordern.

He swung his heels up on the seat, and burrowed a frowsy head into the cushions.

"And that's a' I get", he moaned. "A heid hetter than hell fire, and twae een lookin' different ways for the Sabbath."

"What did it?" I asked.

"A drink they ca' brandy. Bein' a teetotaller I keepit off the whisky, but I was nip-nippin' a' day at this brandy, and I doubt I'll no be weel for a fornicht." His voice died away into a stutter, and sleep once more laid its heady hand on him.

My plan had been to get out at some station down the line, but the train suddenly gave me a better chance, for it came to a standstill at the end of a culvert which spanned a brawling porter-coloured river. I looked out and saw that every carriage window was closed and no human figure appeared in the landscape. So I opened the door, and dropped quickly into the tangle of hazels which edged the line.

It would have been all right but for that infernal dog. Under the impression that I was decamping with its master's belongings, it started to bark, and all but got

1 **to burrow:** vergraben, verbergen.
2 **frowsy:** schmutzig, schlampig, ungepflegt.
3 **heid:** *head.*
hetter: *hotter.*
4 **twae een** (Scot.): *two eyes.*
8 **to nip:** nippen.
10 **stutter:** Stottern.
11 **heady:** ungestüm; berauschend, einlullend.
14 **culvert:** (unterirdischer) Kanal.
15 **porter-coloured:** porter(bier)farben, dunkelbraun.
21 **to decamp:** verschwinden, sich aus dem Staube machen.

me by the trousers. This woke up the herd, who stood bawling at the carriage door in the belief that I had committed suicide. I crawled through the thicket, reached the edge of the stream, and in cover of the bushes put a hundred yards or so behind me. Then from my shelter I peered back, and saw the guard and several passengers gathered round the open carriage door and staring in my direction. I could not have made a more public departure if I had left with a bugler and a brass band.

Happily the drunken herd provided a diversion. He and his dog, which was attached by a rope to his waist, suddenly cascaded out of the carriage, landed on their heads on the track, and rolled some way down the bank towards the water. In the rescue which followed the dog bit somebody, for I could hear the sound of hard swearing. Presently they had forgotten me, and when after a quarter of a mile's crawl I ventured to look back, the train had started again and was vanishing in the cutting.

I was in a wide semicircle of moorland, with the brown river as radius, and the high hills forming the northern circumference. There was not a sign or sound of a hu-

2 **to bawl:** schreien, brüllen.
3 **thicket:** Dickicht.
6 **to peer:** spähen, gucken.
9 **bugler:** Hornist(in).
10 **brass band:** (Blech-)Blaskapelle.
11 **diversion:** Ablenkung.
13 **to cascade:** (heraus)stürzen, fallen.
20 **cutting:** Einschnitt, Durchstich, Graben.
23 **circumference:** Umkreis, Umfang.

man being, only the plashing water and the interminable crying of curlews. Yet, oddly enough, for the first time I felt the terror of the hunted on me. It was not the police that I thought of, but the other folk, who knew that I knew Scudder's secret and dared not let me live. I was certain that they would pursue me with a keenness and vigilance unknown to the British law, and that once their grip closed on me I should find no mercy.

I looked back, but there was nothing in the landscape. The sun glinted on the metals of the line and the wet stones in the stream, and you could not have found a more peaceful sight in the world. Nevertheless I started to run. Crouching low in the runnels of the bog, I ran till the sweat blinded my eyes. The mood did not leave me till I had reached the rim of mountain and flung myself panting on a ridge high above the young waters of the brown river.

From my vantage-ground I could scan the whole moor right away to the railway line and to the south of it where green fields took the place of heather. I have eyes like a hawk, but I could see nothing moving in the whole countryside. Then I looked east beyond the

1 **to plash:** plätschern.
7 **keenness:** Schärfe, Heftigkeit, Eifer.
vigilance: Wachsamkeit.
11 **to glint:** schimmern, glitzern, blinken.
14 **to crouch:** hocken, sich ducken, zusammenkauern.
runnel: Bach, Rinne.
16 **rim:** Rand.
17 **to pant:** keuchen, japsen, schnaufen.
19 **vantage-ground:** günstige Stellung, günstiger Aussichtspunkt.

ridge and saw a new kind of landscape – shallow green valleys with plentiful fir plantations and the faint lines of dust which spoke of highroads. Last of all I looked into the blue May sky, and there I saw that which set my pulses racing. . . .

Low down in the south a monoplane was climbing into the heavens. I was as certain as if I had been told that that aeroplane was looking for me, and that it did not belong to the police. For an hour or two I watched it from a pit of heather. It flew low along the hill-tops, and then in narrow circles over the valley up which I had come. Then it seemed to change its mind, rose to a great height, and flew away back to the south.

I did not like this espionage from the air, and I began to think less well of the countryside I had chosen for a refuge. These heather hills were no sort of cover if my enemies were in the sky, and I must find a different kind of sanctuary. I looked with more satisfaction to the green country beyond the ridge, for there I should find woods and stone houses.

About six in the evening I came out of the moorland to a white ribbon of road which wound up the narrow vale of a lowland stream. As I followed it, fields gave place to bent, the glen became a plateau, and presently I had reached a kind of pass where a solitary house smoked

2 **fir:** Tanne, Fichte.
6 **monoplane:** Eindecker (Flugzeug mit einfachen Tragflächen).
14 **espionage:** Spionage, Ausspionieren.
18 **sanctuary:** Zufluchtsstätte, Asyl.
23 **lowland:** auf das schottische Tiefland bezogen.
24 **bent:** Straußgras, Sandsegge.

in the twilight. The road swung over a bridge, and leaning on the parapet was a young man.

He was smoking a long clay pipe and studying the water with spectacled eyes. In his left hand was a small book with a finger marking the place. Slowly he repeated –

As when a Gryphon through the wilderness
With wingéd step, o'er hill and moory dale
Pursues the Arimaspian.

He jumped round as my step rung on the keystone, and I saw a pleasant sunburnt boyish face.

"Good evening to you," he said gravely. "It's a fine night for the road."

The smell of peat smoke and of some savoury roast floated to me from the house.

"Is that place an inn?" I asked.

"At your service," he said politely. "I am the landlord, sir, and I hope you will stay the night, for to tell you the truth I have had no company for a week."

I pulled myself up on the parapet of the bridge and filled my pipe. I began to detect an ally.

2 **parapet:** (Brücken-)Geländer.

6 f. **"As when a Gryphon through the wilderness / . . . / Pursues the Arimaspian":** John Milton, *Paradise Lost* II,945 f. In dem Versepos von 1667 verläßt Satan seinen »gefallenen« Staat, um mit den Kräften des Chaos und der Nacht Gott herauszufordern (*gryphon:* Greif [Fabeltier]; *dale* [poet.]: Tal; *Arimaspian:* Angehörige[r] des sagenumwobenen Volkes der Arimaspen mit nur einem Auge. Die Arimaspen befanden sich in ständigem Krieg mit den Greifen, deren Gold sie zu stehlen suchten).

13 **peat:** Torf.

savoury: wohlschmeckend, -riechend, appetitlich, würzig, pikant.

20 **ally:** Verbündete(r).

"You're young to be an innkeeper," I said.
"My father died a year ago and left me the business. I live there with my grandmother. It's a slow job for a young man, and it wasn't my choice of profession."
"Which was?"
He actually blushed. "I want to write books," he said.
"And what better chance could you ask?" I cried. "Man, I've often thought that an innkeeper would make the best storyteller in the world."
"Not now," he said eagerly. "Maybe in the old days when you had pilgrims and ballad-makers and highwaymen and mail-coaches on the road. But not now. Nothing comes here but motor-cars full of fat women, who stop for lunch, and a fisherman or two in the spring, and the shooting tenants in August. There is not much material to be got out of that. I want to see life, to travel the world, and write things like Kipling and Conrad. But the most I've done yet is to get some verses printed in *Chamber's Journal.*
I looked at the inn standing golden in the sunset against the brown hills.

11 **pilgrim:** Pilger(in), Wallfahrer(in).
11 f. **highwayman:** Straßenräuber.
15 **shooting tenant:** (Jagd-)Pächter(in), Inhaber(in) von Jagdrechten.
17 **Kipling:** Rudyard K. (1865–1936), englischer Schriftsteller, geboren in Bombay (Indien).
18 **Conrad:** Joseph C., d. i. Jozef Teodor Konrad Korzeniowski (1857 bis 1924), englischer Schriftsteller, geboren als Sohn polnischer Eltern in der von den Russen besetzten Ukraine; wurde 1886 britischer Staatsbürger.
19 **"Chambers's Journal":** Organ der schottischen Volksaufklärung, das 1832 von den aus Peebles (Borders) stammenden Verlegern William und Robert Chambers gegründet wurde.

"I've knocked a bit about the world, and I wouldn't despise such a hermitage. D'you think that adventure is found only in the tropics or among gentry in red shirts? Maybe you're rubbing shoulders with it at this moment."

"That's what Kipling says," he said, his eyes brightening, and he quoted some verse about "Romance bringing up the 9.15".

"Here's a true tale for you then," I cried, "and a month from now you can make a novel out of it."

Sitting on the bridge in the soft May gloaming I pitched him a lovely yarn. It was true in essentials, too, though I altered the minor details. I made out that I was a mining magnate from Kimberley, who had had a lot of trouble with I. D. B. and had shown up a gang. They had pursued me across the ocean, and had killed my best friend, and were now on my tracks.

I told the story well, though I say it who shouldn't. I pictured a flight across the Kalahari to German Africa, the crackling, parching days, the wonderful blue-velvet

2 **hermitage:** Einsiedelei, Klause.

3 **gentry in red shirts:** gemeint sind die Anhänger des italienischen Freiheitskämpfers Giuseppe Garibaldi (1807–82), der in Schottland fünfzig Jahre später immer noch als Held verehrt wurde.

7 f. **Romance . . . 9.15:** Zitat aus Kiplings Gedicht »Romance« (1894).

11 **gloaming** (Scot.): (Abend-)Dämmerung.

14 **Kimberley:** Zentrum des Diamantenabbaus im Oranjefreistaat (Republik Südafrika), gegründet 1870.

15 **I.D.B.:** Abk. für *Illegal Diamond Buying:* illegaler Diamantenankauf; im damaligen Südafrika weit verbreitet.
to show up: bloßstellen, entlarven.

19 **Kalahari:** Wüste in Betschuanaland (Botswana).
German Africa: Deutsch-Südwestafrika (Namibia).

20 **parching:** sengend (Hitze).

nights. I described an attack on my life on the voyage home, and I made a really horrid affair of the Portland Place murder. "You're looking for adventure," I cried; "well, you've found it here. The devils are after me, and the police are after them. It's a race that I mean to win."

"By God!" he whispered, drawing his breath in sharply, "it is all pure Rider Haggard and Conan Doyle."

"You believe me," I said gratefully.

"Of course I do," and he held out his hand. "I believe everything out of the common. The only thing to distrust is the normal."

He was very young, but he was the man for my money.

"I think they're off my track for the moment, but I must lie close for a couple of days. Can you take me in?"

He caught my elbow in his eagerness and drew me towards the house. "You can lie as snug here as if you were in a mosshole. I'll see that nobody blabs, either. And you'll give me some more material about your adventures?"

8 **Rider Haggard:** Sir Henry R. H. (1856–1925), englischer Schriftsteller von Abenteuerromanen, die auch in Afrika spielen.
Conan Doyle: Sir Arthur C. D. (1859–1930), schottischer Schriftsteller, der vor allem durch seine Sherlock-Holmes-Kriminalromane berühmt wurde.
16 **to lie close:** sich versteckt halten.
18 **eagerness:** Eifer, Begierde, Ungeduld.
19 **snug:** geborgen, gut versorgt, behaglich.
20 **mosshole:** Moosmulde.
to blab: schwatzen, quatschen, ausplaudern.

As I entered the inn porch I heard from far off the beat of an engine. There silhouetted against the dusky West was my friend, the monoplane.

He gave me a room at the back of the house, with a fine outlook over the plateau, and he made me free of his own study, which was stacked with cheap editions of his favourite authors. I never saw the grandmother, so I guessed she was bedridden. An old woman called Margit brought me my meals, and the innkeeper was around me at all hours. I wanted some time to myself, so I invented a job for him. He had a motor-bicycle, and I sent him off next morning for the daily paper, which usually arrived with the post in the later afternoon. I told him to keep his eyes skinned, and make note of any strange figures he saw, keeping a special sharp look-out for motors and aeroplanes. Then I sat down in real earnest to Scudder's note-book.

He came back at mid-day with the *Scotsman*. There was nothing in it, except some further evidence of Paddock and the milkman, and a repetition of yesterday's statement that the murderer had gone North. But there was a long article, reprinted from *The Times*, about Karolides and the state of affairs in the Balkans, though there was no mention of any visit to England. I got rid of the innkeeper for the afternoon, for I was getting very warm in my search for the cypher.

1 **porch:** Vordach, (überdachter) Vorbau; Windfang.
2 **dusky:** dämmrig, dunkel.
5 f. **to make s.o. free of s.th.:** jdm. etwas zur Verfügung stellen.
8 **bedridden:** bettlägrig.
14 **to keep one's eyes skinned** (slang): die Augen offenhalten, wie ein Schießhund aufpassen.

As I told you, it was a numerical cypher, and by an elaborate system of experiments I had pretty well discovered what were the nulls and stops. The trouble was the key word, and when I thought of the odd million words he might have used I felt pretty hopeless. But about three o'clock I had a sudden inspiration.

The name Julia Czechenyi flashed across my memory. Scudder had said it was the key to the Karolides business, and it occurred to me to try it on his cypher. It worked. The five letters of "Julia" gave me the position of the vowels. A was J, the tenth letter of the alphabet, and so represented by X in the cypher. E was U = XXI, and so on. "Czechenyi" gave me the numerals for the principal consonants. I scribbled that scheme on a bit of paper and sat down to read Scudder's pages.

In half an hour I was reading with a whitish face and fingers that drummed on the table.

I glanced out of the window and saw a big touring-car coming up the glen towards the inn. It drew up at the door, and there was the sound of people alighting. There seemed to be two of them, men in aquascutums and tweed caps.

Ten minutes later the innkeeper slipped into the room, his eyes bright with excitement.

2 **elaborate:** (wohl)durchdacht, (sorgfältig) ausgearbeitet, ausgeklügelt.
9 **it occurred to me:** es fiel mir ein, es kam mir der Gedanke.
14 **numeral:** Zahl, Ziffer.
to scribble: kritzeln.
19 **touring-car:** Kombi.
22 **aquascutum:** Regenmantel.

"There's two chaps below looking for you," he whispered. "They're in the dining-room having whiskies and sodas. They asked about you and said they had hoped to meet you here. Oh! and they described you jolly well, down to your boots and shirt. I told them you had been here last night and had gone off on a motor-bicycle this morning, and one of the chaps swore like a navvy."

I made him tell me what they looked like. One was a dark-eyed thin fellow with bushy eyebrows, the other was always smiling and lisped in his talk. Neither was any kind of foreigner; on this my young friend was positive.

I took a bit of paper and wrote these words in German as if they were part of a letter –

... Black Stone. Scudder had got on to this, but he could not act for a fortnight. I doubt if I can do any good now, especially as Karolides is uncertain about his plans. But if Mr T. advises I will do the best I ...

I manufactured it rather neatly, so that it looked like a loose page of a private letter.

"Take this down and say it was found in my bedroom, and ask them to return it to me if they overtake me."

Three minutes later I heard the car begin to move, and peeping from behind the curtain caught sight of the two figures. One was slim, the other was sleek; that was the most I could make of my reconnaissance.

8 **navvy:** Kanal-, Erd-, Streckenarbeiter.
19 **to manufacture:** herstellen.
24 **to peep:** (hervor)gucken, neugierig, verstohlen blicken.
25 **sleek:** wohlgenährt; geschmeidig, glatt; gepflegt, elegant, schick.
26 **reconnaissance** (milit.): Erkundung, Aufklärung.

The innkeeper appeared in great excitement. "Your paper woke them up," he said gleefully. "The dark fellow went as white as death and cursed like blazes, and the fat one whistled and looked ugly. They paid for their drinks with half-a-sovereign and wouldn't wait for change."

"Now I'll tell you what I want you to do," I said. "Get on your bicycle and go off to Newton-Stewart to the Chief Constable. Describe the two men, and say you suspect them of having had something to do with the London murder. You can invent reasons. The two will come back, never fear. Not to-night, for they'll follow me forty miles along the road, but first thing to-morrow morning. Tell the police to be here bright and early."

He set off like a docile child, while I worked at Scudder's notes. When he came back we dined together, and in common decency I had to let him pump me. I gave him a lot of stuff about lion hunts and the Matabele War, thinking all the while what tame businesses these were compared to this I was now engaged in. When he went to bed I sat up and finished Scudder. I smoked in a chair till daylight, for I could not sleep.

About eight next morning I witnessed the arrival of two constables and a sergeant. They put their car in a

2 **gleefully** (adv.): ausgelassen, fröhlich; schadenfroh, frohlockend.
3 **like blazes** (infml.): wie verrückt.
5 **half-a-sovereign:** ehemalige 10-Schilling-Münze; entspricht etwa 50 Pence.
9 **Chief Constable:** Polizeipräsident der Grafschaft.
14 **bright and early** (adv.): in aller Frühe.
15 **docile:** fügsam, gelehrig.
17 **decency:** Anstand.

coachhouse under the innkeeper's instructions, and entered the house. Twenty minutes later I saw from my window a second car come across the plateau from the opposite direction. It did not come up to the inn, but stopped two hundred yards off in the shelter of a patch of wood. I noticed that its occupants carefully reversed it before leaving it. A minute or two later I heard their steps on the gravel outside the window.

My plan had been to lie hid in my bedroom, and see what happened. I had a notion that, if I could bring the police and my other more dangerous pursuers together, something might work out of it to my advantage. But now I had a better idea. I scribbled a line of thanks to my host, opened the window, and dropped quietly into a gooseberry bush. Unobserved I crossed the dyke, crawled down the side of a tributary burn, and won the highroad on the far side of the patch of trees. There stood the car, very spick and span in the morning sunlight, but with the dust on her which told of a long journey. I started her, jumped into the chauffeur's seat, and stole gently out on to the plateau.

Almost at once the road dipped so that I lost sight of the inn, but the wind seemed to bring me the sound of angry voices.

5 f. **patch of wood:** Stück Wald.
6 **to reverse:** zurücksetzen, rückwärts fahren.
8 **gravel:** Kies, Schotter.
15 **dyke:** *dike:* Erdwall, erhöhter Fahrdamm; Graben.
16 **tributary:** Nebenfluß.
burn (Scot.): Bach.
18 **spick and span:** funkelnagelneu; blitzblank.
21 **to steal out:** sich davonstehlen.

Chapter IV

The Adventure of the Radical Candidate

You may picture me driving that 40 h. p. car for all she was worth over the crisp moor roads on that shining May morning; glancing back at first over my shoulder, and looking anxiously to the next turning; then driving with a vague eye, just wide enough awake to keep on the highway. For I was thinking desperately of what I had found in Scudder's note-book.

The little man had told me a pack of lies. All his yarns about the Balkans and the Jew-Anarchists and the Foreign Office Conference were eyewash, and so was Karolides. And yet not quite, as you shall hear. I had staked everything on my belief in his story, and had been let down; here was his book telling me a different tale, and instead of being once-bit-twice-shy, I believed it absolutely.

Why, I don't know. It rang desperately true, and the first yarn, if you understand me, had been in a queer way true also in spirit. The fifteenth day of June was going to be a day of destiny, a bigger destiny than the killing of a Dago. It was so big that I didn't blame Scud-

3 **h.p.:** Abk. für *horsepower.*
3 f. **for all she was worth** (infml.): etwa: auf Teufel komm raus.
4 **crisp:** trocken.
12 **eyewash** (fig.): Quatsch, Augenwischerei.
16 **to be once-bit-twice-shy** (infml.): etwa: klüger, vorgewarnt, mißtrauisch sein.
22 **Dago** (pej.): Spanier, Portugiese oder Italiener, Kanake, (verdammter) Ausländer.

der for keeping me out of the game and wanting to play a lone hand. That, I was pretty clear, was his intention. He had told me something which sounded big enough, but the real thing was so immortally big that he, the man who had found it out, wanted it all for himself. I didn't blame him. It was risks after all that he was chiefly greedy about.

The whole story was in the notes – with gaps, you understand, which he would have filled up from his memory. He stuck down his authorities, too, and had an odd trick of giving them all a numerical value and then striking a balance, which stood for the reliability of each stage in the yarn. The four names he had printed were authorities, and there was a man, Ducrosne, who got five out of a possible five; and another fellow, Amersfoort, who got three. The bare bones of the tale were all that was in the book – these, and one queer phrase which occurred half a dozen times inside brackets. "(Thirty-nine steps)" was the phrase; and at its last time of use it ran – "(Thirty-nine steps, I counted them – high tide 10.17 p. m.)". I could make nothing of that.

The first thing I learned was that it was no question of preventing a war. That was coming, as sure as Christ-

1 f. **to play a lone hand** (fig.): einen Alleingang machen.
6 f. **to be greedy about s.th.:** nach etwas gieren.
10 **to stick down** (infml.): hin-, aufschreiben.
12 **to strike a balance:** Bilanz ziehen.
reliability: Verläßlichkeit.
16 **bare bones** (pl.): (fig.) Kern, Gerüst.
18 f. **inside brackets:** in Klammern.
21 **high tide:** höchster Flutwasserstand.

mas: had been arranged, said Scudder, ever since February 1912. Karolides was going to be the occasion. He was booked all right, and was to hand in his checks on June 14th, two weeks and four days from that May morning. I gathered from Scudder's notes that nothing on earth could prevent that. His talk of Epirot guards that would skin their own grandmothers was all billy-o.

The second thing was that this war was going to come as a mighty surprise to Britain. Karolides' death would set the Balkans by the ears, and then Vienna would chip in with an ultimatum. Russia wouldn't like that, and there would be high words. But Berlin would play the peacemaker, and pour oil on the waters, till suddenly she would find a good cause for a quarrel, pick it up, and in five hours let fly at us. That was the idea, and a pretty good one too. Honey and fair speeches, and then a stroke in the dark. While we were talking about the goodwill and good intentions of Germany our coast would be silently ringed with mines, and submarines would be waiting for every battleship.

But all this depended upon the third thing, which was due to happen on June 15th. I would never have grasped this if I hadn't once happened to meet a French staff officer, coming back from West Africa, who had told me a lot of things. One was that, in spite of all the

3 **to hand in one's checks** (AE, infml.): abkratzen, sterben.
8 **billy-o** (infml.): Quatsch.
12 **to chip in with s.th.:** sich mit etwas einmischen; etwas beisteuern.
14 **to pour oil on the waters** (fig.): die Gemüter beruhigen.
20 **submarine:** U-Boot.

nonsense talked in Parliament, there was a real working alliance between France and Britain, and that the two General Staffs met every now and then, and made plans for joint action in case of war. Well, in June a very great swell was coming over from Paris, and he was going to get nothing less than a statement of the disposition of the British Home Fleet on mobilization. At least I gathered it was something like that; anyhow, it was something uncommonly important.

But on the 15th day of June there were to be others in London – others, at whom I could only guess. Scudder was content to call them collectively the "Black Stone". They represented not our Allies, but our deadly foes; and the information, destined for France, was to be diverted to their pockets. And it was to be used, remember – used a week or two later, with great guns and swift torpedoes, suddenly in the darkness of a summer night.

This was the story I had been deciphering in a back room of a country inn, overlooking a cabbage garden.

1 f. **a real working alliance ... Britain:** 1911 hatten bereits Absprachen zwischen Frankreich und Großbritannien stattgefunden, wonach die französische Flotte ins Mittelmeer überwechseln, die britische die deutschen Häfen bewachen und die britische Armee an der linken Flanke der französischen kämpfen sollte.

7 **British Home Fleet:** britische Nordseeflotte.

13 **foe:** Gegner(in), Feind(in).

14 f. **to divert:** umleiten, lenken.

19 **to decipher:** entziffern.

20 **cabbage garden:** Anspielung auf die Autoren des sentimentalen Kailyard (von schott. *kailyard* ›Kohlgarten‹) um Sir James Matthew Barrie (1860–1937). Diese literarische Gruppe verkörperte das engstirnige, provinzielle Schottland, gegen das Buchan sich auflehnte.

This was the story that hummed in my brain as I swung in the big touring-car from glen to glen.

My first impulse had been to write a letter to the Prime Minister, but a little reflection convinced me that that would be useless. Who would believe my tale? I must show a sign, some token in proof, and Heaven knew what that could be. Above all, I must keep going myself, ready to act when things got riper, and that was going to be no light job with the police of the British Isles in full cry after me and the watchers of the Black Stone running silently and swiftly on my trail.

I had no very clear purpose in my journey, but I steered east by the sun, for I remembered from the map that if I went north I would come into a region of coalpits and industrial towns. Presently I was down from the moorlands and traversing the broad haugh of a river. For miles I ran alongside a park wall, and in a break of the trees I saw a great castle. I swung through little old thatched villages, and over peaceful lowland streams,

1 **to hum:** summen.

5 **Who would believe my tale?:** Selbst in seinen Schauerromanen entfernt sich Buchan nie sehr weit von der Bibel. Siehe hierzu Jesaja 53,1: »Aber wer glaubt unsrer Predigt, und wem wird der Arm des Herrn offenbart?« und Markus 8,11 f.: »Und die Pharisäer gingen heraus und fingen an, sich mit ihm zu befragen, versuchten ihn und begehrten von ihm ein Zeichen vom Himmel [. . .]«.

6 **token:** (An-)Zeichen, Merkmal, Beweis.

10 (*to be*) **in full cry after s.o.:** jdn. mit großem Geschrei verfolgen.

12 **to steer:** steuern, lenken.

14 **coalpit:** Kohlegrube.

16 **to traverse:** durch-, überqueren.
haugh (Scot.): Flußaue.

19 **thatched:** stroh-, reetgedeckt.

and past gardens blazing with hawthorn and yellow laburnum. The land was so deep in peace that I could scarcely believe that somewhere behind me were those who sought my life; ay, and that in a month's time, unless I had the almightiest of luck, these round country faces would be pinched and staring, and men would be lying dead in English fields.

About mid-day I entered a long straggling village, and had a mind to stop and eat. Half-way down was the Post Office, and on the steps of it stood the postmistress and a policeman hard at work conning a telegram. When they saw me they wakened up, and the policeman advanced with raised hand, and cried on me to stop.

I nearly was fool enough to obey. Then it flashed upon me that the wire had to do with me; that my friends at the inn had come to an understanding, and were united in desiring to see more of me, and that it had been easy enough for them to wire the description of me and the car to thirty villages through which I might pass. I released the brakes just in time. As it was, the policeman made a claw at the hood, and only dropped off when he got my left in his eye.

I saw that main roads were no place for me, and turned

1 **to blaze:** leuchten, (er)strahlen, lodern.
2 **laburnum:** Goldregen (Zierstrauch).
6 **pinched:** abgehärmt.
8 **to straggle:** sich ausbreiten.
11 **to con:** sorgfältig durchlesen, studieren.
19 **to wire:** telegrafieren.
22 **to make a claw at s.th.:** sich an etwas krallen.
hood: Motorhaube.

into the byways. It wasn't an easy job without a map, for there was the risk of getting on to a farm road and ending in a duck-pond or a stable-yard, and I couldn't afford that kind of delay. I began to see what an ass I had been to steal the car. The big green brute would be the safest kind of clue to me over the breadth of Scotland. If I left it and took to my feet, it would be discovered in an hour or two and I would get no start in the race.

The immediate thing to do was to get to the loneliest roads. These I soon found when I struck up a tributary of the big river, and got into a glen with steep hills all about me, and a corkscrew road at the end which climbed over a pass. Here I met nobody, but it was taking me too far north, so I slewed east along a bad track and finally struck a big double-line railway. Away below me I saw another broadish valley, and it occurred to me that if I crossed it I might find some remote inn to pass the night. The evening was now drawing in, and I was furiously hungry, for I had eaten nothing since breakfast except a couple of buns I had bought from a baker's cart.

Just then I heard a noise in the sky, and lo and behold! there was that infernal aeroplane, flying low, about a dozen miles to the south and rapidly coming towards me.

3 **duck-pond:** Ententeich.
4 **ass:** Esel, Dummkopf.
8 f. **to get no start in the race** (fig.): keine Chance haben.
13 **corkscrew:** Korkenzieher; Spirale.
15 **to slew:** herumdrehen, -schwenken.
21 **bun:** süßes Brötchen.
23 **lo and behold** (hum.): siehe da!

I had the sense to remember that on a bare moor I was at the aeroplane's mercy, and that my only chance was to get to the leafy cover of the valley. Down the hill I went like blue lightning, screwing my head round, whenever I dared, to watch that damned flying machine. Soon I was on a road between hedges, and dipping to the deep-cut glen of a stream. Then came a bit of thick wood where I slackened speed.

Suddenly on my left I heard the hoot of another car, and realized to my horror that I was almost upon a couple of gateposts through which a private road debouched on the highway. My horn gave an agonized roar, but it was too late. I clapped on my brakes, but my impetus was too great, and there before me a car was sliding athwart my course. In a second there would have been the deuce of a wreck. I did the only thing possible, and ran slap into the hedge on the right, trusting to find something soft beyond.

But there I was mistaken. My car slithered through the hedge like butter, and then gave a sickening plunge for-

2 **to be at s.o.'s mercy:** jdm. ausgeliefert sein.
4 **like blue lightning:** blitzschnell, wie ein geölter Blitz.
8 **to slacken:** (Tempo) verlangsamen, herabsetzen.
9 **hoot:** Hupen.
11 **gatepost:** Torpfosten.
11 f. **to debouch on s.th.:** in etwas einmünden.
12 **agonized:** qualvoll, herzzerreißend.
13 **to clap on s.th.:** hier: hastig, heftig auf etwas treten.
14 **impetus:** Schwung, Triebkraft.
15 **athwart:** quer, schräg hindurch.
17 **slap** (adv., infml.): voll, genau, direkt, mit voller Wucht.
19 **to slither:** schlittern, rutschen, gleiten.
20 **plunge:** Sprung, Satz, Sturz.

ward. I saw what was coming, leapt on the seat and would have jumped out. But a branch of hawthorn got me in the chest, lifted me up and held me, while a ton or two of expensive metal slipped below me, bucked and pitched, and then dropped with an almighty smash fifty feet to the bed of the stream.

Slowly that thorn let me go. I subsided first on the hedge and then very gently on a bower of nettles. As I scrambled to my feet a hand took me by the arm, and a sympathetic and badly scared voice asked me if I were hurt.

I found myself looking at a tall young man in goggles and a leather ulster, who kept on blessing his soul and whinnying apologies. For myself, once I got my wind back, I was rather glad than otherwise. This was one way of getting rid of the car.

"My blame, sir," I answered him. "It's lucky that I did not add homicide to my follies. That's the end of my Scotch motor tour, but it might have been the end of my life."

4 **to buck:** bocken, sich aufbäumen.
5 **to pitch:** mit einem Ruck nach vorn kippen.
7 **to subside:** (herunter)sinken, absacken.
8 **bower:** schattiges Plätzchen, (Garten-)Laube.
nettle: Brennessel.
9 **to scramble to one's feet:** sich aufrappeln.
12 **goggles** (pl.): Schutzbrille.
13 **ulster:** Ulstermantel, schwerer Herrenmantel, zuerst in der nordirischen Provinz Ulster hergestellt.
14 **to whinny:** wiehern.
14 f. **to get one's wind back:** wieder zu Atem kommen.
18 **homicide:** Mord, Totschlag.
folly: Verrücktheit, Narrheit.

He plucked out a watch and studied it. "You're the right sort of fellow," he said. "I can spare a quarter of an hour, and my house is two minutes off. I'll see you clothed and fed and snug in bed. Where's your kit, by the way? Is it in the burn along with the car?"

"It's in my pocket," I said, brandishing a tooth-brush. "I'm a Colonial and travel light."

"A Colonial," he cried. "By God, you're the very man I've been praying for. Are you by any blessed chance a Free Trader?"

"I am", said I, without the foggiest notion of what he meant.

He patted my shoulder and hurried me into his car. Three minutes later we drew up before a comfortable-looking shooting box set among pine-trees, and he ushered me indoors. He took me first to a bedroom and flung half a dozen of his suits before me, for my own had been pretty well reduced to rags. I selected a loose blue serge, which differed most conspicuously from my former garments, and borrowed a linen collar. Then he haled me to the dining-room, where the remnants of a meal stood on the table, and announced that I had just

4 **kit:** Gepäck, Ausrüstung, Zeug, Sachen.
6 **to brandish:** schwenken; (drohend) schwingen.
10 **Free Trader:** Anhänger(in) des internationalen Freihandels ohne Beschränkungen seitens der Regierung.
11 **without the foggiest notion:** ohne jeden blassen Schimmer.
13 **to pat:** tätscheln.
15 **shooting box:** Jagdhütte.
pine-tree: Kiefer.
15 f. **to usher:** (herein-, hinein)führen, geleiten.
19 **serge:** Serge (Stoff).
21 **to hale** (poet.): zerren, nötigen.

five minutes to feed. "You can take a snack in your pocket, and we'll have supper when we get back. I've got to be at the Masonic Hall at eight o'clock, or my agent will comb my hair."

I had a cup of coffee and some cold ham, while he yarned away on the hearth-rug.

"You find me in the deuce of a mess, Mr — ; by-the-by, you haven't told me your name. Twisdon? Any relation of old Tommy Twisdon of the Sixtieth? No? Well, you see I'm Liberal Candidate for this part of the world, and I had a meeting on to-night at Brattleburn – that's my chief town, and an infernal Tory stronghold. I had got the Colonial ex-Premier fellow, Crumpleton, coming to speak for me to-night, and had the thing tremendously billed and the whole place groundbaited. This afternoon I had a wire from the ruffian saying he had got influenza at Blackpool, and here am I left to do the

3 **Masonic:** Freimaurer-.
4 **to comb s.o.'s hair** (infml.): jdn. ‚auseinandernehmen'.
6 **to yarn:** (fig.) Garn spinnen, Geschichten erzählen.
hearth-rug: Kaminvorleger.
9 **Sixtieth:** Regimentsnummer.
10 **Liberal:** Angehörige(r), Anhänger(in) der liberalen Partei Großbritanniens.
11 **Brattleburn:** fiktiver Name für Lockerbie in Dumfries.
12 **Tory:** Angehörige(r), Anhänger(in) der konservativen Partei Großbritanniens.
stronghold: Hochburg.
15 **to bill:** (durch Plakate) ankündigen.
to groundbait: hier (fig.): etwa: mit Ködern auslegen.
16 **ruffian:** Rüpel, Raufbold.
17 **influenza:** Grippe.
Blackpool: Seebad in der Grafschaft Lancashire an der Westküste Englands.

whole thing myself. I had meant to speak for ten minutes and must now go on for forty, and, though I've been racking my brains for three hours to think of something, I simply cannot last the course. Now you've got to be a good chap and help me. You're a Free Trader and can tell our people what a wash-out Protection is in the Colonies. All you fellows have the gift of the gab – I wish to heaven I had it. I'll be for evermore in your debt."

I had very few notions about Free Trade one way or the other, but I saw no other chance to get what I wanted. My young gentleman was far too absorbed in his own difficulties to think how odd it was to ask a stranger who had just missed death by an ace and had lost a 1000-guinea car to address a meeting for him on the spur of the moment. But my necessities did not allow me to contemplate oddnesses or to pick and choose my supports.

"All right," I said. "I'm not much good as a speaker, but I'll tell them a bit about Australia."

3 **to rack one's brains:** sich den Kopf zerbrechen.

6 **wash-out** (slang): Pleite, Reinfall.

6 f. **protection:** Protektionismus (Schutz der einheimischen Produktion etwa durch die Erhebung von Schutzzöllen auf Importe).

12 **to be absorbed in s.th.:** von etwas in Anspruch genommen sein.

14 **by an ace** (fig.): um Haaresbreite.

15 **1000-guinea:** etwa 100 000 DM (*guinea:* Guinee, britische Goldmünze bis 1813 im Wert von 21 Schilling; auch später noch gebräuchliche Rechnungseinheit).

15 f. **on the spur of the moment:** der Eingebung des Augenblicks folgend, spontan.

20 **Australia:** Australien wurde 1901 zu dem australischen Staatenbund zusammengeschlossen und erhielt 1908 die erste Labour-Regierung

At my words the cares of the ages slipped from his shoulders, and he was rapturous in his thanks. He lent me a big driving coat – and never troubled to ask why I had started on a motor tour without possessing an ulster – and, as we slipped down the dusty roads, poured into my ears the simple facts of his history. He was an orphan, and his uncle had brought him up – I've forgotten the uncle's name, but he was in the Cabinet, and you can read his speeches in the papers. He had gone round the world after leaving Cambridge, and then, being short of a job, his uncle had advised politics. I gathered that he had no preference in parties. "Good chaps in both," he said cheerfully, "and plenty of blighters, too. I'm Liberal, because my family have always been Whigs." But if he was lukewarm politically he had strong views on other things. He found out I knew a bit about horses, and jawed away about the Derby entries; and he was full of plans for improving his shooting. Altogether, a very clean, decent, callow young man.

As we passed through a little town two policemen signalled us to stop, and flashed their lanterns on us.

des britischen Weltreichs unter dem ehemaligen schottischen Kohlegrubenarbeiter Andrew Fisher. Die Labour-Partei (Arbeiterpartei) hatte Schutzzölle bereits gegen rasch wechselnde liberale und Koalitionsregierungen unter schottischer Führung durchgesetzt.

2 **rapturous:** hingerissen, begeistert, verzückt.

7 **orphan:** Waise.

13 **blighter:** Mistkerl, Knülch.

15 **Whig:** Angehörige(r), Anhänger(in) der liberalen Partei; Gegenstück zu Tory.

lukewarm: lauwarm, lau.

17 **to jaw** (slang): quatschen, tratschen.

19 **callow:** ‚grün', unerfahren, unreif.

"Beg pardon, Sir Harry," said one. "We've got instructions to look out for a car, and the description's no unlike yours."

"Right-o," said my host, while I thanked Providence for the devious ways I had been brought to safety. After that he spoke no more, for his mind began to labour heavily with his coming speech. His lips kept muttering, his eye wandered, and I began to prepare myself for a second catastrophe. I tried to think of something to say myself, but my mind was dry as a stone. The next thing I knew we had drawn up outside a door in a street, and were being welcomed by some noisy gentlemen with rosettes.

The hall had about five hundred in it, women mostly, a lot of bald heads, and a dozen or so young men. The chairman, a weaselly minister with a reddish nose, lamented Crumpleton's absence, soliloquized on his influenza, and gave me a certificate as a "trusted leader of Australian thought". There were two policemen at the door, and I hoped they took note of that testimonial. Then Sir Harry started.

I never heard anything like it. He didn't begin to know how to talk. He had about a bushel of notes from which

4 **Providence:** göttliche Vorsehung.
5 **devious:** abwegig, gewunden.
7 **to mutter:** murmeln.
13 **rosette:** Rosette (Wahlplakette, -anstecker).
16 **weaselly:** wieselartig.
16 f. **to lament s.th.:** etwas beklagen.
17 **to soliloquize:** monologisieren; ein Selbstgespräch führen.
20 f. **testimonial:** (Führungs-)Zeugnis, Empfehlung(sschreiben); Zeichen der Anerkennung, Ehrengabe.
23 **bushel:** Scheffel.

he read, and when he let go of them he fell into one prolonged stutter. Every now and then he remembered a phrase he had learned by heart, straightened his back, and gave it off like Henry Irving, and the next moment he was bent double and crooning over his papers. It was the most appalling rot, too. He talked about the "German menace", and said it was all a Tory invention to cheat the poor of their rights and keep back the great flood of social reform, but that "organized labour" realized this and laughed the Tories to scorn. He was all for reducing our Navy as a proof of our good faith, and then sending Germany an ultimatum telling her to do the same or we would knock her into a cocked hat. He said that, but for the Tories, Germany and Britain would be fellow-workers in peace and reform. I thought of the little black book in my pocket! A giddy lot Scudder's friends cared for peace and reform.

Yet in a queer way I liked the speech. You could see the niceness of the chap shining out behind the muck with which he had been spoon-fed. Also it took a load off my mind. I mightn't be much of an orator, but I was a thousand per cent better than Sir Harry.

4 **Irving:** Henry I. (1838–1905), britischer Theaterdirektor, der selbst ziemlich gekünstelt Rollen spielte.
5 **to croon:** leise, schmachtend singen; summen, murmeln.
6 **appalling:** entsetzlich.
10 **to laugh s.o. to scorn:** jdn. verlachen.
13 f. **to knock s.o. into a cocked hat:** jdn. zu Brei schlagen, restlos fertigmachen.
20 **muck** (infml.): Mist.
21 **to spoon-feed s.o.** (fig.): jdm. etwas vorkauen, eintrichtern.
22 **orator:** Redner(in).

I didn't get on so badly when it came to my turn. I simply told them all I could remember about Australia, praying there should be no Australian there – all about its labour party and emigration and universal service. I doubt if I remembered to mention Free Trade, but I said there were no Tories in Australia, only Labour and Liberals. That fetched a cheer, and I woke them up a bit when I started in to tell them the kind of glorious business I thought could be made out of the Empire if we really put our backs into it.

Altogether I fancy I was rather a success. The minister didn't like me, though, and when he proposed a vote of thanks, spoke of Sir Harry's speech as "statesmanlike" and mine as having "the eloquence of an emigration agent".

When we were in the car again my host was in wild spirits at having got his job over. "A ripping speech, Twisdon," he said. "Now, you're coming home with me. I'm all alone, and if you'll stop a day or two I'll show you some very decent fishing."

We had a hot supper – and I wanted it pretty badly – and then drank grog in a big cheery smoking-room with a crackling wood fire. I thought the time had come for me to put my cards on the table. I saw by this man's eye that he was the kind you can trust.

"Listen, Sir Harry," I said. "I've something pretty important to say to you. You're a good fellow, and I'm go-

10 **to put one's back into s.th.** (fig.): sich mit aller Kraft für etwas einsetzen.

14 **eloquence:** Beredtheit.

17 **ripping** (slang): prächtig, prima, toll.

ing to be frank. Where on earth did you get that poisonous rubbish you talked to-night?"

His face fell. "Was it as bad as that?" he asked ruefully. "It did sound rather thin. I got most of it out of the *Progressive Magazine* and pamphlets that agent chap of mine keeps sending me. But you surely don't think Germany would ever go to war with us?"

"Ask that question in six weeks and it won't need an answer," I said. "If you'll give me your attention for half an hour I am going to tell you a story."

I can see yet that bright room with the deers' heads and the old prints on the walls, Sir Harry standing restlessly on the stone curb of the hearth, and myself lying back in an armchair, speaking. I seemed to be another person, standing aside and listening to my own voice, and judging carefully the reliability of my tale. It was the first time I had ever told anyone the exact truth, so far as I understood it, and it did me no end of good, for it straightened out the thing in my own mind. I blinked no detail. He heard all about Scudder, and the milkman, and the note-book, and my doings in Galloway. Presently he got very excited and walked up and down the hearth-rug.

"So you see," I concluded, "you have got here in your house the man that is wanted for the Portland Place

3 **ruefully** (adv.): kläglich, jämmerlich; wehmütig, reumütig.

5 **"Progressive Magazine":** fiktiver Name; vermutl. Anspielung auf die politische Zeitschrift *Progressive Review* (1895–97), von deren Autoren Buchan einige kannte.
pamphlet: Broschüre; Flugblatt.

13 **curb:** Randstein, Kante.

19 **to blink s.th.:** etwas ignorieren.

murder. Your duty is to send your car for the police and give me up. I don't think I'll get very far. There'll be an accident, and I'll have a knife in my ribs an hour or so after arrest. Nevertheless it's your duty, as a law-abiding citizen. Perhaps in a month's time you'll be sorry, but you have no cause to think of that."

He was looking at me with bright steady eyes. "What was your job in Rhodesia, Mr Hannay?" he asked.

"Mining engineer," I said. "I've made my pile cleanly and I've had a good time in the making of it."

"Not a profession that weakens the nerves, is it."

I laughed. "Oh, as to that, my nerves are good enough." I took down a hunting-knife from a stand on the wall, and did the old Mashona trick of tossing it and catching it in my lips. That wants a pretty steady heart.

He watched me with a smile. "I don't want proof. I may be an ass on the platform, but I can size up a man. You're no murderer and you're no fool, and I believe you are speaking the truth. I'm going to back you up. Now, what can I do?"

"First, I want you to write a letter to your uncle. I've got to get in touch with the Government people sometime before the 15th of June."

He pulled his moustache. "That won't help you. This is Foreign Office business, and my uncle would have nothing to do with it. Besides, you'd never convince

4 f. **law-abiding:** gesetzestreu, ordnungsliebend.

14 **Mashona:** Maschona, Eingeborene von Südrhodesien (Simbabwe); im Gegensatz zu den Matabele ein friedliches, scheues Volk.
to toss: werfen, schleudern.

18 **to size up s.o.** (infml.): jdn. einschätzen, taxieren.

him. No, I'll go one better. I'll write to the Permanent Secretary at the Foreign Office. He's my godfather, and one of the best going. What do you want?

He sat down at a table and wrote to my dictation. The gist of it was that if a man called Twisdon (I thought I had better stick to that name) turned up before June 15th he was to entreat him kindly. He said Twisdon would prove his *bona fides* by passing the word "Black Stone" and whistling "Annie Laurie".

"Good," said Sir Harry. "That's the proper style. By the way, you'll find my godfather – his name's Sir Walter Bullivant – down at his country cottage for Whitsuntide. It's close to Artinswell on the Kennet. That's done. Now, what's the next thing?"

"You're about my height. Lend me the oldest tweed suit you've got. Anything will do, so long as the colour is the opposite of the clothes I destroyed this afternoon. Then show me a map of the neighbourhood and explain to me the lie of the land. Lastly, if the police come seeking me, just show them the car in the glen. If the other lot turn up, tell them I caught the south express after your meeting."

1 **to go one better:** (fig.) einen Schritt weitergehen.
1 f. **Permanent Secretary:** ständiger fachlicher Staatssekretär.
2 **godfather:** Pate; Patenonkel.
7 **to entreat** (arch.): behandeln.
8 **bona fides** (Lat.): guter Glaube, Treu und Glauben; ehrliche Absicht, Rechtmäßigkeit.
12 f. **Whitsuntide:** Pfingsten.
13 **Artinswell:** fiktiver Name; vermutl. Anspielung auf Aldermaston in der Grafschaft Berkshire westlich von London.
Kennet: Fluß in Berkshire.
19 **lie of the land:** (geographische) Lage; (fig.) Lage der Dinge.

He did, or promised to do, all these things. I shaved off the remnants of my moustache, and got inside an ancient suit of what I believe is called heather mixture. The map gave me some notion of my whereabouts, and told me the two things I wanted to know – where the main railway to the south could be joined and what were the wildest districts near at hand.

At two o'clock he wakened me from my slumbers in the smoking-room armchair, and led me blinking into the dark starry night. An old bicycle was found in a tool-shed and handed over to me.

"First turn to the right up by the long fir-wood," he enjoined. "By daybreak you'll be well into the hills. Then I should pitch the machine into a bog and take to the moors on foot. You can put in a week among the shepherds, and be as safe as if you were in New Guinea."

I pedalled diligently up steep roads of hill gravel till the skies grew pale with morning. As the mists cleared before the sun, I found myself in a wide green world with glens falling on every side and a far-away blue horizon. Here, at any rate, I could get early news of my enemies.

12 f. **to enjoin:** einschärfen.
14 **to pitch:** kippen, schleudern, werfen.
17 **diligently** (adv.): fleißig, emsig.

Chapter V

The Adventure of the Spectacled Roadman

I sat down on the very crest of the pass and took stock of my position.

Behind me was the road climbing through a long cleft in the hills, which was the upper glen of some notable river. In front was a flat space of maybe a mile, all pitted with bog-holes and rough with tussocks, and then beyond it the road fell steeply down another glen to a plain whose blue dimness melted into the distance. To left and right were round-shouldered green hills as smooth as pancakes, but to the south – that is, the left hand – there was a glimpse of high heathery mountains, which I remembered from the map as the big knot of hill which I had chosen for my sanctuary. I was on the central boss of a huge upland country, and could see everything moving for miles. In the meadows below the road half a mile back a cottage smoked, but it was the only sign of human life. Otherwise there was only the calling of plovers and the tinkling of little streams.

It was now about seven o'clock, and as I waited I heard once again that ominous beat in the air. Then I realized

3 **crest:** Kamm, Bergrücken, Gipfel.
3 f. **to take stock of s.th.:** über etwas Bilanz ziehen, von etwas Bestandsaufnahme machen.
5 **cleft:** Spalte, Kluft, Riß.
8 **tussock:** (Gras-)Büschel.
16 **boss:** Buckel.
20 **tinkling:** Geklingel, Klingen.
22 **ominous:** ominös, beunruhigend.

that my vantage-ground might be in reality a trap. There was no cover for a tomtit in those bald green places.

I sat quite still and hopeless while the beat grew louder. Then I saw an aeroplane coming up from the east. It was flying high, but as I looked it dropped several hundred feet and began to circle round the knot of hill in narrowing circles, just as a hawk wheels before it pounces. Now it was flying very low, and now the observer on board caught sight of me. I could see one of the two occupants examining me through glasses. Suddenly it began to rise in swift whorls, and the next I knew it was speeding eastward again till it became a speck in the blue morning.

That made me do some savage thinking. My enemies had located me, and the next thing would be a cordon round me. I didn't know what force they could command, but I was certain it would be sufficient. The aeroplane had seen my bicycle, and would conclude that I would try to escape by the road. In that case there might be a chance on the moors to the right or left. I wheeled the machine a hundred yards from the highway, and plunged it into a moss-hole, where it sank among pond-weed and water-buttercups. Then I

2 **tomtit:** (Blau-)Meise.
9 **to pounce:** herabstoßen (Raubvogel).
12 **whorl:** Windung.
14 **speck:** Fleck, Pünktchen.
16 **cordon:** Kordon, Posten-, Absperrkette.
23 **to plunge:** stürzen, stoßen.
24 **pond-weed:** Laichkraut.
water-buttercup: Sumpfdotterblume.

climbed to a knoll which gave me a view of the two valleys. Nothing was stirring on the long white ribbon that threaded them.

I have said there was not cover in the whole place to hide a rat. As the day advanced it was flooded with soft fresh light till it had the fragrant sunniness of the South African veld. At other times I would have liked the place, but now it seemed to suffocate me. The free moorlands were prison walls, and the keen hill air was the breath of a dungeon.

I tossed a coin – heads right, tails left – and it fell heads, so I turned to the north. In a little I came to the brow of the ridge which was the containing wall of the pass. I saw the highroad for maybe ten miles, and far down it something that was moving, and that I took to be a motor-car. Beyond the ridge I looked on a rolling green moor, which fell away into wooded glens.

Now my life on the veld has given me the eyes of a kite, and I can see things for which most men need a telescope. ... Away down the slope, a couple of miles away, several men were advancing like a row of beaters at a shoot. ...

I dropped out of sight behind the skyline. That way was shut to me, and I must try the bigger hills to the south beyond the highway. The car I had noticed was getting

1 **knoll:** Hügel, Kuppe.
6 **fragrant:** wohlriechend, duftend; (fig.) angenehm, köstlich.
8 **to suffocate:** ersticken.
10 **dungeon:** Kerker.
12 **brow:** (Berg-)Kuppe.
18 **kite:** Milan, Gabelweihe.
21 **beater:** (Jagd-)Treiber(in).

nearer, but it was still a long way off with some very steep gradients before it. I ran hard, crouching low except in the hollows, and as I ran I kept scanning the brow of the hill before me. Was it imagination, or did I see figures – one, two, perhaps more – moving in a glen beyond the stream?

If you are hemmed in on all sides in a patch of land there is only one chance of escape. You must stay in the patch, and let your enemies search it and not find you. That was good sense, but how on earth was I to escape notice in that table-cloth of a place? I would have buried myself to the neck in mud or lain below water or climbed the tallest tree. But there was not a stick of wood, the bog-holes were little puddles, the stream was a slender trickle. There was nothing but short heather, and bare hill bent, and the white highway.

Then in a tiny bight of road, beside a heap of stones, I found the roadman.

He had just arrived, and was wearily flinging down his hammer. He looked at me with a fishy eye and yawned.

"Confoond the day I ever left the herdin'!" he said, as if to the world at large. "There I was my ain maister.

2 **gradient:** Steigung.
7 **to hem s.o. in:** jdn. einschließen, umgeben.
14 **puddle:** Pfütze, Lache.
15 **trickle:** Rinnsal.
17 **bight:** Bucht, Einbuchtung, Krümmung.
20 **fishy eye:** (fig.) Fischauge.
22 **confoond:** *confound:* zum Teufel mit …
23 **ain:** *own.*

Now I'm a slave to the Government, tethered to the roadside, wi' sair een, and a back like a suckle."

He took up the hammer, struck a stone, dropped the implement with an oath, and put both hands to his ears. "Mercy on me! My heid's burstin'!" he cried.

He was a wild figure, about my own size but much bent, with a week's beard on his chin, and a pair of big horn spectacles.

"I canna dae't," he cried again. "The Surveyor maun just report me. I'm for my bed."

I asked him what was the trouble, though indeed that was clear enough.

"The trouble is that I'm no sober. Last nicht my dochter Merran was waddit, and they danced till fower in the byre. Me and some ither chiels sat down to the drinkin', and here I am. Peety that I ever lookit on the wine when it was red!"

I agreed with him about bed.

"It's easy speakin'," he moaned. "But I got a post-caird yestreen sayin' that the new Road Surveyor would be round the day. He'll come and he'll no find me, or else he'll find me fou, and either way I'm a done man. I'll awa' back to my bed and say I'm no weel, but I doot

1 **to tether:** an-, festbinden.
2 **sair** (Scot.): *sore:* wund, entzündet.
suckle (Scot.): *sickle:* Sichel.
4 **implement:** Werkzeug, Gerät.
14 **waddit:** *wedded.*
fower: *four.*
15 **byre:** Kuhstall.
ither: *other.*
chiel (Scot.): Mann.
23 **doot:** *doubt.*

that'll no help me, for they ken my kind o' no-weelness."

Then I had an inspiration. "Does the new Surveyor know you?" I asked.

"No him. He's just been a week at the job. He rins about in a wee motor-cawr, and wad speir the inside oot o' a whelk."

"Where's your house?" I asked, and was directed by a wavering finger to the cottage by the stream.

"Well, back to your bed," I said, "and sleep in peace. I'll take on your job for a bit and see the Surveyor."

He stared at me blankly; then, as the notion dawned on his fuddled brain, his face broke into the vacant drunkard's smile.

"You're the billy," he cried. "It'll be easy eneuch managed. I've finished that bing o' stanes, so you needna chap ony mair this forenoon. Just take the barry, and wheel eneuch metal frae yon quarry doon the road to mak anither bing the morn. My name's Alexander

1 **ken** (Scot.): *know.*
6 **wee** (Scot.): klein.
speir (Scot.): Frage.
7 **whelk:** Wellhornschnecke.
13 **fuddled** (infml.): benebelt, verwirrt, betrunken.
13 f. **drunkard:** Trinker(in).
15 **billy:** Kerl.
eneuch: *enough.*
16 **bing** (Scot.): Haufen.
17 **to chap:** *chip:* abbrechen, -schlagen.
ony mair: *any more.*
barry (Scot.): *barrow:* (Hand-, Schub-)Karre.
18 **frae** (Scot.): *from.*
yon (dial.): jene(r, -s) dort.
quarry: Steinbruch.

Turnbull, and I've been seeven year at the trade, and twenty afore that herdin' on Leithen Water. My freens ca' me Ecky, and whiles Specky, for I wear glesses, being weak i' the sicht. Just you speak the Surveyor fair, and ca' him Sir, and he'll be fell pleased. I'll be back or mid-day."

I borrowed his spectacles and filthy old hat; stripped off coat, waistcoat, and collar, and gave him them to carry home; borrowed, too, the foul stump of a clay pipe as an extra property. He indicated my simple tasks, and without more ado set off at an amble bedwards. Bed may have been his chief object, but I think there was also something left in the foot of a bottle. I prayed that he might be safe under cover before my friends arrived on the scene.

Then I set to work to dress for the part. I opened the collar of my shirt – it was a vulgar blue-and-white check such as ploughmen wear – and revealed a neck as brown as any tinker's. I rolled up my sleeves, and there was a forearm which might have been a blacksmith's, sunburnt and rough with old scars. I got my boots and trouser-legs all white from the dust of the road, and hitched up my trousers, tying them with string below the knee. Then I set to work on my face. With a handful of dust I made a water-mark round my neck, the

2 **Leithen Water:** vermutl. Nebenfluß des Tweed in der schottischen Grafschaft Borders.
11 **amble:** gemächlicher Gang, Schlendern.
18 **ploughman:** Pflüger.
19 **tinker:** Kesselflicker.
20 **blacksmith:** Schmied.
23 **to hitch up one's trousers:** den Hosenbund hochziehen.

place where Mr Turnbull's Sunday ablutions might be expected to stop. I rubbed a good deal of dirt also into the sunburn of my cheeks. A roadman's eyes would no doubt be a little inflamed, so I contrived to get some dust in both of mine, and by dint of vigorous rubbing produced a bleary effect.

The sandwiches Sir Harry had given me had gone off with my coat, but the roadman's lunch, tied up in a red handkerchief, was at my disposal. I ate with great relish several of the thick slabs of scone and cheese and drank a little of the cold tea. In the handkerchief was a local paper tied with string and addressed to Mr Turnbull – obviously meant to solace his mid-day leisure. I did up the bundle again, and put the paper conspicuously beside it.

My boots did not satisfy me, but by dint of kicking among the stones I reduced them to the granite-like surface which marks a roadman's foot-gear. Then I bit and scraped my finger-nails till the edges were all cracked and uneven. The men I was matched against would miss no detail. I broke one of the bootlaces and retied it in a clumsy knot, and loosed the other so that my thick grey socks bulged over the uppers. Still no

1 **ablution:** (kirchliche) Waschung; (hum.) Wäsche.
5 **by dint of:** kraft, vermöge, mittels.
6 **bleary:** verschwommen, trübe.
9 **relish:** Genuß, Wonne, Behagen.
10 **slab:** (dickes) Stück, (dicke) Scheibe.
13 **to solace:** trösten.
18 **foot-gear:** Schuhwerk.
23 **to bulge:** sich wölben.
uppers (pl.): Oberleder (Schuhe).

sign of anything on the road. The motor I had observed half an hour ago must have gone home.

My toilet complete, I took up the barrow and began my journeys to and from the quarry a hundred yards off. I remember an old scout in Rhodesia, who had done many queer things in his day, once telling me that the secret of playing a part was to think yourself into it. You could never keep it up, he said, unless you could manage to convince yourself that you were *it*. So I shut off all other thoughts and switched them on to the road-mending. I thought of the little white cottage as my home, I recalled the years I had spent herding on Leithen Water, I made my mind dwell lovingly on sleep in a box-bed and a bottle of cheap whisky. Still nothing appeared on that long white road.

Now and then a sheep wandered off the heather to stare at me. A heron flapped down to a pool in the stream and started to fish, taking no more notice of me than if I had been a milestone. On I went, trundling my loads of stone, with the heavy step of the professional. Soon I grew warm, and the dust on my face changed into solid and abiding grit. I was already counting the

5 **an old scout in Rhodesia:** gemeint ist Peter Pienaar, ein burischer Pfadfinder im Dienst der Briten, der auch in *Greenmantle* (1916) und *Mr Standfast* (1919) vorkommt.

12 **to recall s.th.:** sich an etwas erinnern.

14 **box-bed:** Doppelbett in den sehr beengten Häusern der einfachen Leute Schottlands. Es war in die Wand des oftmals einzigen Raumes eingelassen und mit einem Vorhang abgetrennt.

17 **heron:** Reiher.
to flap: flattern.

19 **to trundle:** fahren, rollen.

22 **abiding:** dauerhaft, hartnäckig.
grit: Sand.

hours till evening should put a limit to Mr Turnbull's monotonous toil.

Suddenly a crisp voice spoke from the road, and looking up I saw a little Ford two-seater, and a round-faced young man in a bowler hat.

"Are you Alexander Turnbull?" he asked. "I am the new County Road Surveyor. You live at Blackhopefoot, and have charge of the section from Laidlawbyres to the Riggs? Good! A fair bit of road, Turnbull, and not badly engineered. A little soft about a mile off, and the edges want cleaning. See you look after that. Good morning. You'll know me the next time you see me."

Clearly my get-up was good enough for the dreaded Surveyor. I went on with my work, and as the morning grew towards noon I was cheered by a little traffic. A baker's van breasted the hill, and sold me a bag of ginger biscuits which I stowed in my trouser-pockets against emergencies. Then a herd passed with sheep, and disturbed me somewhat by asking loudly, "What had become o' Specky?"

"In bed wi' the colic," I replied, and the herd passed on. . . .

Just about mid-day a big car stole down the hill, glided past and drew up a hundred yards beyond. Its three occupants descended as if to stretch their legs, and sauntered towards me.

3 **crisp:** klar, scharf.
7 f. **Blackhopefoot / Laidlawbyres / the Riggs:** vermutl. fiktive Ortsnamen.
13 **get-up:** Aufmachung, Aufzug, Kleidung.
16 **to breast s.th.:** gegen etwas ankämpfen, etwas mühsam bewältigen.
17 **ginger:** Ingwer.

Two of the men I had seen before from the window of the Galloway inn – one lean, sharp, and dark, the other comfortable and smiling. The third had the look of a countryman – a vet, perhaps, or a small farmer. He was dressed in ill-cut knickerbockers, and the eye in his head was as bright and wary as a hen's.

"Morning," said the last. "That's a fine easy job o' yours."

I had not looked up on their approach, and now, when accosted, I slowly and painfully straightened my back, after the manner of roadmen; spat vigorously, after the manner of the low Scot; and regarded them steadily before replying. I confronted three pairs of eyes that missed nothing.

"There's waur jobs and there's better," I said sententiously. "I wad rather hae yours, sittin' a' day on your hinderlands on thae cushions. It's you and your muckle cawrs that wreck my roads! If we a' had oor richts, ye sud be made to mend what ye break."

The bright-eyed man was looking at the newspaper lying beside Turnbull's bundle.

"I see you get your papers in good time," he said.

I glanced at it casually. "Aye, in gude time. Seein' that that paper cam' out last Setterday I'm just sax days late."

4 **vet:** Kurzform von *veterinary surgeon:* Tierarzt, -ärztin.
6 **wary:** wachsam, umsichtig, argwöhnisch.
10 **to accost s.o.:** an jdn. herantreten, jdn. ansprechen.
15 **waur** (Scot.): *worse.*
15 f. **sententiously** (adv.): lehrhaft, salbungsvoll.
17 **hinderlands** (Scot., pl.): Hinterteil, Gesäß.
muckle (Scot.): *mickle:* groß.

He picked it up, glanced at the supersription, and laid it down again. One of the others had been looking at my boots, and a word in German called the speaker's attention to them.

"You've a fine taste in boots," he said. "These were never made by a country shoemaker."

"They were not," I said readily. "They were made in London. I got them frae the gentleman that was here last year for the shootin'. What was his name now?" And I scratched a forgetful head.

Again the sleek one spoke in German. "Let us get on," he said. "This fellow is all right."

They asked one last question.

"Did you see anyone pass early this morning? He might be on a bicycle or he might be on foot."

I very nearly fell into the trap and told a story of a bicyclist hurrying past in the grey dawn. But I had the sense to see my danger. I pretended to consider very deeply.

"I wasna up very early," I said. "Ye see, my dochter was merrit last nicht, and we keepit it up late. I opened the house door about seeven and there was naebody on the road then. Since I cam' up here there has just been the baker and the Ruchill herd, besides you gentlemen."

One of them gave me a cigar, which I smelt gingerly and stuck in Turnbull's bundle. They got into their car and were out of sight in three minutes.

My heart leaped with an enormous relief, but I went on wheeling my stones. It was as well, for ten minutes later

1 **superscription:** Überschrift.
25 **gingerly** (adv.): sachte, behutsam; zimperlich.

the car returned, one of the occupants waving a hand to me. Those gentry left nothing to chance.

I finished Turnbull's bread and cheese, and pretty soon I had finished the stones. The next step was what puzzled me. I could not keep up this roadmaking business for long. A merciful Providence had kept Mr Turnbull indoors, but if he appeared on the scene there would be trouble. I had a notion that the cordon was still tight around the glen, and that if I walked in any direction I should meet with questioners. But get out I must. No man's nerve could stand more than a day of being spied on.

I stayed at my post till about five o'clock. By that time I had resolved to go down to Turnbull's cottage at nightfall and take my chance of getting over the hills in the darkness. But suddenly a new car came up the road, and slowed down a yard or two from me. A fresh wind had risen, and the occupant wanted to light a cigarette.

It was a touring-car, with the tonneau full on an assortment of baggage. One man sat in it, and by an amazing chance I knew him. His name was Marmaduke Jopley, and he was an offence to creation. He was a sort of blood stockbroker, who did his business by toadying el-

20 **tonneau:** hinterer Teil eines Autos.

20 f. **assortment:** Auswahl, Reihe.

22 **Marmaduke Jopley:** Jopleys Nachname in der zuerst in *Blackwood's Magazine* (Literaturzeitschrift in Edinburgh von 1817 bis 1980) veröffentlichten Serienversion des Romans, Mark-Brown, wurde möglicherweise geändert, weil sich jemand beleidigt fühlte.

24 **stockbroker:** Börsenmakler(in).
to toady s.o.: vor jdm. kriechen, scharwenzeln.

dest sons and rich young peers and foolish old ladies. "Marmie" was a familiar figure, I understood, at balls and polo-weeks and country houses. He was an adroit scandal-monger, and would crawl a mile on his belly to anything that had a title or a million. I had a business introduction to his firm when I came to London, and he was good enough to ask me to dinner at his club. There he showed off at a great rate, and pattered about his duchesses till the snobbery of the creature turned me sick. I asked a man afterwards why nobody kicked him, and was told that Englishmen reverenced the weaker sex.

Anyhow there he was now, nattily dressed, in a fine new car, obviously on his way to visit some of his smart friends. A sudden daftness took me, and in a second I had jumped into the tonneau and had him by the shoulder.

"Hullo, Jopley," I sang out. "Well met, my lad!" He got a horrid fright. His chin dropped as he stared at me. "Who the devil are you?" he gasped.

"My name's Hannay," I said. "From Rhodesia, you remember."

"Good God, the murderer!" he choked.

"Just so. And there'll be a second murder, my dear, if you don't do as I tell you. Give me that coat of yours. That cap, too."

1 **peer:** Angehöriger des britischen Hochadels; Mitglied des Oberhauses.
3 **adroit:** geschickt, gewandt, schlagfertig, pfiffig.
3 f. **scandal-monger:** Lästermaul, Klatschbase.
8 **to patter about s.th.:** Sprüche über etwas klopfen.
11 **to reverence:** (ver)ehren.
12 **nattily** (adv.): schick, piekfein (angezogen), elegant.

He did as bid, for he was blind with terror. Over my dirty trousers and vulgar shirt I put on his smart driving-coat, which buttoned high at the top and thereby hid the deficiencies of my collar. I stuck the cap on my head, and added his gloves to my get-up. The dusty roadman in a minute was transformed into one of the neatest motorists in Scotland. On Mr Jopley's head I clapped Turnbull's unspeakable hat, and told him to keep it there.

Then with some difficulty I turned the car. My plan was to go back the road he had come, for the watchers, having seen it before, would probably let it pass unremarked, and Marmie's figure was in no way like mine.

"Now, my child," I said, "sit quite still and be a good boy. I mean you no harm. I'm only borrowing your car for an hour or two. But if you play me any tricks, and above all if you open your mouth, as sure as there's a God above me I'll wring your neck. *Savez*?"

I enjoyed that evening's ride. We ran eight miles down the valley, through a village or two, and I could not help noticing several strange-looking folk lounging by the roadside. These were the watchers who would have had much to say to me if I had come in other garb or company. As it was, they looked incuriously on. One touched his cap in salute, and I responded graciously.

As the dark fell I turned up a side glen which, as I remembered from the map, led into an unfrequented cor-

19 **savez?** (Fr.): verstehen Sie?, verstanden?
24 **garb:** Tracht, Gewand.
25 **incuriously** (adv.): desinteressiert.

ner of the hills. Soon the villages were left behind, then the farms, and then even the wayside cottage. Presently we came to a lonely moor where the night was blackening the sunset gleam in the bog pools. Here we stopped, and I obligingly reversed the car and restored to Mr Jopley his belongings.

"A thousand thanks," I said. "There's more use in you than I thought. Now be off and find the police."

As I sat on the hillside, watching the tail-light dwindle, I reflected on the various kinds of crime I had now sampled. Contrary to general belief, I was not a murderer, but I had become an unholy liar, a shameless impostor, and a highwayman with a marked taste for expensive motor-cars.

Chapter VI

The Adventure of the Bald Archaeologist

I spent the night on a shelf of the hillside, in the lee of a boulder where the heather grew long and soft. It was a cold business, for I had neither coat nor waistcoat.

2 **wayside:** am Wegrand.
4 **gleam:** Glanz.
5 **obligingly** (adv.): gefällig, zuvorkommend.
9 **tail-light:** Rücklicht, Rückfahrscheinwerfer.
to dwindle: (ver)schwinden (Licht).
12 f. **impostor:** Betrüger(in), Schwindler(in), Hochstapler(in).
17 **shelf:** Felsplatte.
lee: Windschattenseite, windgeschützte Stelle.
18 **boulder:** Felsbrocken.

These were in Mr Turnbull's keeping, as was Scudder's little book, my watch and – worst of all – my pipe and tobacco pouch. Only my money accompanied me in my belt, and about half a pound of ginger biscuits in my trousers pocket.

I supped off half those biscuits, and by worming myself deep into the heather got some kind of warmth. My spirits had risen, and I was beginning to enjoy this crazy game of hide-and-seek. So far I had been miraculously lucky. The milkman, the literary innkeeper, Sir Harry, the roadman, and the idiotic Marmie, were all pieces of undeserved good fortune. Somehow the first success gave me a feeling that I was going to pull the thing through.

My chief trouble was that I was desperately hungry. When a Jew shoots himself in the City and there is an inquest, the newspapers usually report that the deceased was "well-nourished". I remember thinking that they would not call me well-nourished if I broke my neck in a bog-hole. I lay and tortured myself – for the ginger biscuits merely emphasized the aching void – with the memory of all the good food I had thought so little of in London. There were Paddock's crisp sausages and fragrant shavings of bacon, and shapely poached eggs – how often I had turned up my nose at

6 **to sup off s.th.** (arch.): etwas zu Abend essen.
to worm o.s.: sich schlängeln.
9 **hide-and-seek:** Versteckspiel.
21 **void:** (Gefühl der) Leere.
23 **crisp:** knackig.
24 **shavings** (pl.): Schnitzel, Stückchen, Streifen.
25 **poached egg:** pochiertes, verlorenes Ei.

them! There were the cutlets they did at the club, and a particular ham that stood on the cold table, for which my soul lusted. My thoughts hovered over all varieties of mortal edible, and finally settled on a porterhouse steak and a quart of bitter with a welsh rabbit to follow. In longing hopelessly for these dainties I fell asleep.

I woke very cold and stiff about an hour after dawn. It took me a while to remember where I was, for I had been very weary and had slept heavily. I saw first the pale blue sky through a net of heather, then a big shoulder of hill, and then my own boots placed neatly in a blaeberry bush. I raised myself on my arms and looked down into the valley, and that one look set me lacing up my boots in mad haste.

For there were men below, not more than a quarter of a mile off, spaced out on the hillside like a fan, and beating the heather. Marmie had not been slow in looking for his revenge.

I crawled out of my shelf into the cover of a boulder, and from it gained a shallow trench which slanted up

1 **cutlet:** Kotelett, Schnitzel.
2 f. **to lust for s.th.:** nach etwas gieren.
3 **to hover:** schweben, fliegen.
4 **edible:** Eßbares; Nahrungsmittel.
4 f. **porterhouse steak:** Rindersteak.
5 **quart:** Hohlmaß; 1 quart entspricht 1,136 l.
welsh rabbit: Käsetoast.
6 **dainty:** Delikatesse, Leckerbissen.
10 f. **shoulder:** Vorsprung; Randstreifen.
12 **blaeberry** (Scot.): Heidelbeere.
17 **to beat s.th.:** sich einen Weg durch etwas bahnen.
20 **trench:** Graben.
to slant: schräg verlaufen.

the mountain face. This led me presently into the narrow gully of a burn, by way of which I scrambled to the top of the ridge. From there I looked back, and saw that I was still undiscovered. My pursuers were patiently quartering the hillside and moving upwards. Keeping behind the skyline I ran for maybe half a mile, till I judged I was above the uppermost end of the glen. Then I showed myself, and was instantly noted by one of the flankers, who passed the word to the others. I heard cries coming up from below, and saw that the line of search had changed its direction. I pretended to retreat over the skyline, but instead went back the way I had come, and in twenty minutes was behind the ridge overlooking my sleeping place. From that viewpoint I had the satisfaction of seeing the pursuit streaming up the hill at the top of the glen on a hopelessly false scent.

I had before me a choice of routes, and I chose a ridge which made an angle with the one I was on, and so would soon put a deep glen between me and my enemies. The exercise had warmed my blood, and I was beginning to enjoy myself amazingly. As I went I breakfasted on the dusty remnants of the ginger biscuits.

I knew very little about the country, and I hadn't a notion what I was going to do. I trusted to the strength of my legs, but I was well aware that those behind me would be familiar with the lie of the land, and that my

2 **gully:** Wasserrinne.
5 **to quarter:** durchqueren, -stöbern, -kämmen.
9 **flanker** (milit.): Flanke, Seitenpatrouille.

ignorance would be a heavy handicap. I saw in front of me a sea of hills, rising very high towards the south, but northwards breaking down into broad ridges which separated wide and shallow dales. The ridge I had chosen seemed to sink after a mile or two to a moor which lay like a pocket in the uplands. That seemed as good a direction to take as any other.

My strategem had given me a fair start – call it twenty minutes – and I had the width of a glen behind me before I saw the first heads of the pursuers. The police had evidently called in local talent to their aid, and the men I could see had the appearance of herds or gamekeepers. They hallooed at the sight of me, and I waved my hand. Two dived into the glen and began to climb my ridge, while the others kept their own side of the hill. I felt as if I were taking part in a schoolboy game of hare and hounds.

But very soon it began to seem less of a game. Those fellows behind were hefty men on their native heath. Looking back I saw that only three were following direct, and I guessed that the others had fetched a circuit to cut me off. My lack of local knowledge might very well be my undoing, and I resolved to get out of this tangle of glens to the pocket of moor I had seen from

1 **ignorance:** Unwissenheit, Unkenntnis.
8 **strategem:** (Kriegs-)List.
12 f. **gamekeeper:** Wildheger, -hüter.
17 **hare and hounds:** Schnitzeljagd.
19 **hefty:** kräftig, stämmig.
heath: Heide(land).
21 **to fetch:** einnehmen, ausführen.
23 **undoing:** Unglück, Verderben, Ruin.
24 **pocket:** Kessel, Loch, Mulde, Senke.

the tops. I must so increase my distance as to get clear away from them, and I believed I could do this if I could find the right ground for it. If there had been cover I would have tried a bit of stalking, but on these bare slopes you could see a fly a mile off. My hope must be in the length of my legs and the soundness of my wind, but I needed easier ground for that, for I was not bred a mountaineer. How I longed for a good Afrikander pony!

I put on a great spurt and got off my ridge and down into the moor before any figures appeared on the skyline behind me. I crossed a burn, and came out on a highroad which made a pass between two glens. All in front of me was a big field of heather sloping up to a crest which was crowned with an odd feather of trees. In the dyke by the roadside was a gate, from which a grass-grown track led over the first wave of the moor.

I jumped the dyke and followed it, and after a few hundred yards – as soon as it was out of sight of the highway – the grass stopped and it became a very respectable road, which was evidently kept with some care. Clearly it ran to a house, and I began to think of doing the same. Hitherto my luck had held, and it might be that my best chance would be found in this remote

4 **stalking:** Pirsch(jagd) (*to stalk:* pirschen).
8 **mountaineer:** Bergsteiger(in).
8 f. **Afrikander:** weißer Einwohner der Republik Südafrika mit Afrikaans als Muttersprache; auch: südafrikanische Rinder- bzw. Schafsrasse.
15 f. **feather of trees:** kleine, fiedrig wirkende Baumgruppe.
24 **hitherto** (adv.): bisher, bis jetzt.

dwelling. Anyhow there were trees there, and that meant cover.

I did not follow the road, but the burnside which flanked it on the right, where the bracken grew deep and the high banks made a tolerable screen. It was well I did so, for no sooner had I gained the hollow than, looking back, I saw the pursuit topping the ridge from which I had descended.

After that I did not look back; I had no time. I ran up the burnside, crawling over the open places, and for a large part wading in the shallow stream. I found a deserted cottage with a row of phantom peat stacks and an overgrown garden. Then I was among young hay, and very soon had come to the edge of a plantation of wind-blown firs. From there I saw the chimneys of the house smoking a few hundred yards to my left. I forsook the burnside, crossed another dyke, and almost before I knew was on a rough lawn. A glance back told me that I was well out of sight of the pursuit, which had not yet passed the first lift of the moor.

The lawn was a very rough place, cut with a scythe instead of a mower, and planted with beds of scrubby rhododendrons. A brace of black-game, which are not

4 **bracken:** Farnkraut.
11 **to wade:** waten.
12 **stack:** Stapel, Stoß.
16 f. **to forsake:** verlassen, aufgeben.
21 **scythe:** Sense.
22 **mower:** Rasenmäher.
scrubby: verkümmert, krüppelhaft (Strauch).
23 **a brace:** ein Paar, zwei.
black-game: Birkhuhn.

usually garden birds, rose at my approach. The house before me was the ordinary moorland farm, with a more pretentious white-washed wing added. Attached to this wing was a glass veranda, and through the glass I saw the face of an elderly gentleman meekly watching me.

I stalked over the border of coarse hill gravel and entered the open veranda door. Within was a pleasant room, glass on one side, and on the other a mass of books. More books showed in an inner room. On the floor, instead of tables, stood cases such as you see in a museum, filled with coins and queer stone implements.

There was a knee-hole desk in the middle, and seated at it, with some papers and open volumes before him, was the benevolent old gentleman. His face was round and shiny, like Mr Pickwick's, big glasses were stuck on the end of his nose, and the top of his head was as bright and bare as a glass bottle. He never moved when I entered, but raised his placid eyebrows and waited on me to speak.

It was not an easy job, with about five minutes to spare, to tell a stranger who I was and what I wanted, and to

3 **pretentious:** protzig.
white-washed: weiß getüncht, verputzt.
5 **meekly** (adv.): mild, sanftmütig; demütig, fromm.
14 **knee-hole desk:** Schreibtisch mit Öffnung für die Knie.
16 **benevolent:** wohltätig, gutmütig, wohlwollend.
17 **Mr Pickwick:** Mr Samuel Pickwick, kauzig-gutmütiger Charakter aus Charles Dickens' Roman *The Posthumous Papers of the Pickwick Club* (1837).
20 **placid:** ruhig, gelassen.

win his aid. I did not attempt it. There was something about the eye of the man before me, something so keen and knowledgeable, that I could not find a word. I simply stared at him and stuttered.

"You seem in a hurry, my friend," he said slowly.

I nodded towards the window. It gave a prospect across the moor through a gap in the plantation, and revealed certain figures half a mile off straggling through the heather.

"Ah, I see," he said, and took up a pair of field-glasses through which he patiently scrutinized the figures.

"A fugitive from justice, eh? Well, we'll go into the matter at our leisure. Meantime I object to my privacy being broken in upon by the clumsy rural policeman. Go into my study, and you will see two doors facing you. Take the one on the left and close it behind you. You will be perfectly safe."

And this extraordinary man took up his pen again.

I did as I was bid, and found myself in a little dark chamber which smelt of chemicals, and was lit only by a tiny window high up in the wall. The door had swung behind me with a click like the door of a safe. Once again I had found an unexpected sanctuary.

All the same I was not comfortable. There was something about the old gentleman which puzzled and rather terrified me. He had been too easy and ready, almost as if he had expected me. And his eyes had been horribly intelligent.

11 **to scrutinize:** genau prüfen, untersuchen, ansehen, studieren.
12 **fugitive:** Flüchtige(r), Flüchtling.
13 **privacy:** Privatsphäre.

No sound came to me in that dark place. For all I knew the police might be searching the house, and if they did they would want to know what was behind this door. I tried to possess my soul in patience, and to forget how hungry I was.

Then I took a more cheerful view. The old gentleman could scarcely refuse me a meal, and I fell to reconstructing my breakfast. Bacon and eggs would content me, but I wanted the better part of a flitch of bacon and half a hundred eggs. And then, while my mouth was watering in anticipation, there was a click and the door stood open.

I emerged into the sunlight to find the master of the house sitting in a deep armchair in the room he called his study, and regarding me with curious eyes.

"Have they gone?" I asked.

"They have gone. I convinced them that you had crossed the hill. I do not choose that the police should come between me and one whom I am delighted to honour. This is a lucky morning for you, Mr Richard Hannay."

As he spoke his eyelids seemed to tremble and to fall a little over his keen grey eyes. In a flash the phrase of Scudder's came back to me, when he had described the man he most dreaded in the world. He had said that he "could hood his eyes like a hawk". Then I saw that I had walked straight into the enemy's headquarters.

My first impulse was to throttle the old ruffian and

9 **flitch of bacon:** Speckseite.
11 **in anticipation:** im voraus.
28 **to throttle:** erwürgen.

make for the open air. He seemed to anticipate my intention, for he smiled gently, and nodded to the door behind me.

I turned, and saw two men-servants who had me covered with pistols.

He knew my name, but he had never seen me before. And as the reflexion darted across my mind I saw a slender chance.

"I don't know what you mean," I said roughly. "And who are you calling Richard Hannay? My name's Ainslie."

"So?" he said, still smiling. "But of course you have others. We won't quarrel about a name."

I was pulling myself together now, and I reflected that my garb, lacking coat and waistcoat and collar, would at any rate not betray me. I put on my surliest face and shrugged my shoulders.

"I suppose you're going to give me up after all, and I call it a damned dirty trick. My God, I wish I had never seen that cursed motor-car! Here's the money and be damned to you," and I flung four sovereigns on the table.

He opened his eyes a little. "Oh no, I shall not give you up. My friends and I will have a little private settlement with you, that is all. You know a little too much, Mr Hannay. You are a clever actor, but not quite clever enough."

He spoke with assurance, but I could see the dawning of a doubt in his mind.

16 **surly:** verdrießlich, mürrisch, bärbeißig.
17 **to shrug one's shoulders:** die Schultern, Achseln zucken.

"Oh, for God's sake stop jawing," I cried. "Everything's against me. I haven't had a bit of luck since I came on shore at Leith. What's the harm in a poor devil with an empty stomach picking up some money he finds in a bust-up motor-car? That's all I done, and for that I've been chivvied for two days by those blasted bobbies over those blasted hills. I tell you I'm fair sick of it. You can do what you like, old boy! Ned Ainslie's got no fight left in him."

I could see that the doubt was gaining.

"Will you oblige me with the story of your recent doings?" he asked.

"I can't, guv'nor," I said in a real beggar's whine. "I've not had a bite to eat for two days. Give me a mouthful of food, and then you'll hear God's truth."

I must have showed my hunger in my face, for he signalled to one of the men in the doorway. A bit of cold pie was brought and a glass of beer, and I wolfed them down like a pig – or rather, like Ned Ainslie, for I was keeping up my character. In the middle of my meal he spoke suddenly to me in German, but I turned on him a face as blank as a stone wall.

Then I told him my story – how I had come off an Archangel ship at Leith a week ago, and was making my way overland to my brother at Wigtown. I had run

5 **bust-up:** kaputt, ruiniert.
6 **to chivvy s.o.:** jdn. herumjagen, hetzen, schikanieren.
7 **blasted:** verflucht.
13 **whine:** jammernder Ton, Gejammer.
18 **pie:** (Fleisch-, Obst-)Pastete.
18 f. **to wolf s.th. down:** etwas (gierig) verschlingen.
24 **Archangel:** Archangelsk, Hafenstadt im Nordwesten Rußlands.
25 **Wigtown:** Ort an der Südküste von Galloway.

short of cash – I hinted vaguely at a spree – and I was pretty well on my uppers when I had come on a hole in a hedge, and, looking through, had seen a big motor-car lying in the burn. I had poked about to see what had happened, and had found three sovereigns lying on the seat and one on the floor. There was nobody there or any sign of an owner, so I had pocketed the cash. But somehow the law had got after me. When I had tried to change a sovereign in a baker's shop, the woman had cried on the police, and a little later, when I was washing my face in a burn, I had been nearly gripped, and had only got away by leaving my coat and waistcoat behind me.

"They can have the money back," I cried, "for a fat lot of good it's done me. Those perishers are all down on a poor man. Now, if it had been you, guv'nor, that had found the quids, nobody would have troubled you."

"You're a good liar, Hannay," he said.

I flew into a rage. "Stop fooling, damn you! I tell you my name's Ainslie, and I never heard of anyone called Hannay in my born days. I'd sooner have the police than you with your Hannays and your monkey-faced pistol tricks. . . . No, guv'nor, I beg pardon, I don't mean that. I'm much obliged to you for the grub, and I'll thank you to let me go now the coast's clear."

1 **spree:** Sauftour; (Kauf-)Orgie.
1 f. **to be well on one's uppers** (infml.): auf dem trocknen sitzen, total abgebrannt, auf dem Hund sein.
4 **to poke about:** herumtasten, -tappen, -stöbern.
15 **perisher:** (kleiner) Räuber (Kind).
22 f. **monkey-faced trick** (slang): krumme Tour, fauler Zauber.
24 **grub** (slang): Futter, Essen.
25 **the coast's clear** (fig.): die Luft ist rein, die Bahn ist frei.

It was obvious that he was badly puzzled. You see he had never seen me, and my appearance must have altered considerably from my photographs, if he had got one of them. I was pretty smart and well dressed in London, and now I was a regular tramp.

"I do not propose to let you go. If you are what you say you are, you will soon have a chance of clearing yourself. If you are what I believe you are, I do not think you will see the light much longer."

He rang a bell, and a third servant appeared from the veranda.

"I want the Lanchester in five minutes," he said. "There will be three to luncheon."

Then he looked steadily at me, and that was the hardest ordeal of all.

There was something weird and devilish in those eyes, cold, malignant, unearthly, and most hellishly clever. They fascinated me like the bright eyes of a snake. I had a strong impulse to throw myself on his mercy and offer to join his side, and if you consider the way I felt about the whole thing you will see that that impulse must have been purely physical, the weakness of a brain mesmerized and mastered by a stronger spirit. But I managed to stick it out and even to grin.

"You'll know me next time, guv'nor," I said.

"Karl," he spoke in German to one of the men in the doorway, "you will put this fellow in the storeroom till

12 **Lanchester:** wahrsch. fortschrittlichstes Auto der damaligen Zeit.
15 **ordeal:** (fig.) Zerreißprobe, Feuerprobe, schwere Prüfung, Tortur.
16 **weird:** unheimlich.
17 **malignant:** böswillig, arglistig, (heim)tückisch, gehässig.
23 **to mesmerize:** (fig.) faszinieren, bannen.

I return, and you will be answerable to me for his keeping."

I was marched out of the room with a pistol at each ear.

The storeroom was a damp chamber in what had been the old farmhouse. There was no carpet on the uneven floor, and nothing to sit down on but a school form. It was black as pitch, for the windows were heavily shuttered. I made out by groping that the walls were lined with boxes and barrels and sacks of some heavy stuff. The whole place smelt of mould and disuse. My gaolers turned the key in the door, and I could hear them shifting their feet as they stood on guard outside.

I sat down in that chilly darkness in a very miserable frame of mind. The old boy had gone off in a motor to collect the two ruffians who had interviewed me yesterday. Now, they had seen me as the roadman, and they would remember me, for I was in the same rig. What was a roadman doing twenty miles from his beat, pursued by the police? A question or two would put them on the track. Probably they had seen Mr Turnbull, probably Marmie too; most likely they could link me up with Sir Harry, and then the whole thing would be crystal clear. What chance had I in this moorland

1 **to be answerable to s.o. for s.th.:** jdm. für etwas bürgen, sich vor jdm. für etwas verantworten müssen.
6 **form:** (Schul-)Bank.
7 **pitch:** Pech.
8 **to grope:** tasten.
10 **mould:** Moder.
gaoler: (Gefängnis-)Aufseher(in), -wärter(in).
18 **beat:** Gebiet, Revier.

house with three desperadoes and their armed servants?

I began to think wistfully of the police, now plodding over the hills after my wraith. They at any rate were fellow-countrymen and honest men, and their tender mercies would be kinder than these ghoulish aliens. But they wouldn't have listened to me. That old devil with the eyelids had not taken long to get rid of them. I thought he probably had some kind of graft with the constabulary. Most likely he had letters from Cabinet Ministers saying he was to be given every facility for plotting against Britain. That's the sort of owlish way we run our politics in the Old Country.

The three would be back for lunch, so I hadn't more than a couple of hours to wait. It was simply waiting on destruction, for I could see no way out of this mess. I wished that I had Scudder's courage, for I am free to confess I didn't feel any great fortitude. The only thing that kept me going was that I was pretty furious. It made me boil with rage to think of those three spies

3 **wistfully** (adv.): sehnsüchtig, wehmütig, versonnen.
to plod: schwerfällig gehen, sich dahinschleppen, trotten, (einher) stapfen.

4 **wraith:** Geistererscheinung (besonders von gerade Gestorbenen), Geist, Gespenst.

6 **ghoulish:** ghulenhaft (*ghul:* leichenverzehrender Dämon), greulich, makaber.
alien: Fremde(r), Außerirdische(r).

9 **graft** (infml.): Gaunerei, Schieberei; (AE) Vorteilsnahme, Bestechungsgeschäft.

10 **constabulary:** Polizei(truppe).

12 **owlish:** eulenhaft; (fig.) weise, neunmalklug.

18 **fortitude:** innere Stärke, Kraft.

getting the pull on me like this. I hoped that at any rate I might be able to twist one of their necks before they downed me.

The more I thought of it the angrier I grew, and I had to get up and move about the room. I tried the shutters, but they were the kind that lock with a key, and I couldn't move them. From the outside came the faint clucking of hens in the warm sun. Then I groped among the sacks and boxes. I couldn't open the latter, and the sacks seemed to be full of things like dog-biscuits that smelt of cinnamon. But, as I circumnavigated the room, I found a handle in the wall which seemed worth investigating.

It was the door of a wall cupboard – what they call a "press" in Scotland – and it was locked. I shook it, and it seemed rather flimsy. For want of something better to do I put out my strength on that door, getting some purchase on the handle by looping my braces round it. Presently the thing gave with a crash which I thought would bring in my warders to inquire. I waited for a bit, and then started to explore the cupboard shelves.

There was a multitude of queer things there. I found an

1 **to get the pull on s.o.** (slang): Macht über jdn. erlangen.
8 **clucking:** Gackern, Glucken.
11 **cinnamon:** Zimt.
to circumnavigate s.th.: etwas durchqueren, in etwas herumgehen.
16 **flimsy:** hauchdünn, zart, schwach, leicht.
18 **purchase:** Hebelkraft, Hebelwirkung, (guter) Angriffs-, Ansatzpunkt.
to loop: schlingen.
braces (pl.): Hosenträger.
20 **warder:** Wärter.

odd vesta or two in my trouser pockets and struck a light. It went out in a second, but it showed me one thing. There was a little stock of electric torches on one shelf. I picked up one, and found it was in working order.

With a torch to help me I investigated further. There were bottles and cases of queer-smelling stuffs, chemicals no doubt for experiments, and there were coils of fine copper wire and yanks and yanks of a thin oiled silk. There was a box of detonators, and a lot of cord for fuses. Then away at the back of a shelf I found a stout brown cardboard box, and inside it a wooden case. I managed to wrench it open, and within lay half a dozen little grey bricks, each a couple of inches square.

I took up one, and found that it crumbled easily in my hand. Then I smelt it and put my tongue to it. After that I sat down to think. I hadn't been a mining engineer for nothing, and I knew lentonite when I saw it.

With one of these bricks I could blow the house to smithereens. I had used the stuff in Rhodesia and knew its power. But the trouble was that my knowledge wasn't exact. I had forgotten the proper charge and the

1 **vesta:** Kurzform von *vesta match:* kurzes Streichholz.
8 **coil:** Rolle, Spirale, Knäuel.
9 **yank:** gemeint ist vermutl. *hank:* Knäuel, Strang.
10 **detonator:** Zünd-, Sprengkapsel.
11 **fuse:** (Zeit-)Zünder; Zündschnur.
13 **to wrench s.th. open:** etwas aufreißen.
16 **to crumble:** zerbröckeln, -krümeln, -fallen.
19 **lentonite:** fiktive Sprengstoffart, die dazu dienen soll, die Tür aufzusprengen, ohne Hannay mit in die Luft zu sprengen.
20 f. **to blow s.th. to smithereens:** etwas in tausend Stücke zerfetzen.

right way of preparing it, and I wasn't sure about the timing. I had only a vague notion, too, as to its power, for though I had used it I had not handled it with my own fingers.

But it was a chance, the only possible chance. It was a mighty risk, but against it was an absolute black certainty. If I used it the odds were, as I reckoned, about five to one in favour of my blowing myself into the tree-tops; but if I didn't I should very likely be occupying a six-foot hole in the garden by the evening. That was the way I had to look at it. The prospect was pretty dark either way, but anyhow there was a chance, both for myself and for my country.

The remembrance of little Scudder decided me. It was about the beastliest moment of my life, for I'm no good at these cold-blooded resolutions. Still I managed to rake up the pluck to set my teeth and choke back the horrid doubts that flooded in on me. I simply shut off my mind and pretended I was doing an experiment as simple as Guy Fawkes fireworks.

I got a detonator, and fixed it to a couple of feet of fuse. Then I took a quarter of a lentonite brick, and buried it near the door below one of the sacks in a crack of the floor, fixing the detonator in it. For all I knew half those boxes might be dynamite. If the cupboard held

17 **to rake up:** (fig.) wieder ausgraben, aufbringen.
pluck: Mut.
to set one's teeth: (fig.) die Zähne zusammenbeißen.

20 **Fawkes:** Guy F. (um 1570–1606) englischer Verschwörer; der Jahrestag der Aufdeckung des Gunpowder Plot (Pulververschwörung in London im Jahre 1605) wird bis heute in Großbritannien am 5. November mit Feuerwerk gefeiert.

such deadly explosives, why not the boxes? In that case there would be a glorious skyward journey for me and the German servants and about an acre of the surrounding country. There was also the risk that the detonation might set off the other bricks in the cupboard, for I had forgotten most that I knew about lentonite. But it didn't do to begin thinking about the possibilities. The odds were horrible, but I had to take them.

I ensconced myself just below the sill of the window, and lit the fuse. Then I waited for a moment or two. There was dead silence – only a shuffle of heavy boots in the passage, and the peaceful cluck of hens from the warm out-of-doors. I commended my soul to my Maker, and wondered where I would be in five seconds. . . .

A great wave of heat seemed to surge upwards from the floor, and hang for a blistering instant in the air. Then the wall opposite me flashed into a golden yellow and dissolved with a rending thunder that hammered my brain into a pulp. Something dropped on me, catching the point of my left shoulder.

And then I think I became unconscious.

My stupor can scarcely have lasted beyond a few seconds. I felt myself being choked by thick yellow fumes,

9 **sill:** Fensterbrett.
11 **shuffle:** Schlurfen.
14 **Maker:** Schöpfer, Gott.
17 **blistering:** glühend heiß; erbittert, mörderisch.
19 **rending:** (Stille) zerreißend.
20 **pulp:** Brei.
23 **stupor:** Benommenheit, Betäubung.
24 **fumes:** Dämpfe, Rauch.

and struggled out of the debris to my feet. Somewhere behind me I felt fresh air. The jambs of the window had fallen, and through the ragged rent the smoke was pouring out to the summer noon. I stepped over the broken lintel, and found myself standing in a yard in a dense and acrid fog. I felt very sick and ill, but I could move my limbs, and I staggered blindly forward away from the house.

A small mill-lade ran in a wooden aqueduct at the other side of the yard, and into this I fell. The cool water revived me, and I had just enough wits left to think of escape. I squirmed up the lade among the slippery green slime till I reached the mill-wheel. Then I wriggled through the axle hole into the old mill and tumbled on to a bed of chaff. A nail caught the seat of my trousers, and I left a wisp of heather-mixture behind me.

The mill had been long out of use. The ladders were rotten with age, and in the loft the rats had gnawed great holes in the floor. Nausea shook me, and a wheel

1 **debris:** Trümmer, Schutt.
2 **jamb:** (Tür-, Fenster-)Pfosten.
3 **rent:** Riß, Spalte.
5 **lintel:** (Tür-, Fenster-)Sturz.
6 **acrid:** (fig.) scharf, ätzend, beißend.
9 **mill-lade** (Scot.): Mühlbach.
aqueduct: Rinne, (Wasser-)Leitung.
12 **to squirm:** sich krümmen, winden.
13 f. **to wriggle:** sich winden, schlängeln.
14 **axle:** (Rad-)Achse.
15 **chaff:** Spreu, Häcksel.
16 **wisp:** (Stroh-, Heu-)Büschel.
19 **to gnaw:** nagen, knabbern.
20 **nausea:** Übelkeit.

in my head kept turning, while my left shoulder and arm seemed to be stricken with the palsy. I looked out of the window and saw a fog still hanging over the house and smoke escaping from an upper window. Please God I had set the place on fire, for I could hear confused cries coming from the other side.

But I had no time to linger, since this mill was obviously a bad hiding-place. Anyone looking for me would naturally follow the lade, and I made certain the search would begin as soon as they found that my body was not in the storeroom. From another window I saw that on the far side of the mill stood an old stone dovecot. If I could get there without leaving tracks I might find a hiding-place, for I argued that my enemies, if they thought I could move, would conclude I had made for open country, and would go seeking me on the moor.

I crawled down the broken ladder, scattering chaff behind me to cover my footsteps. I did the same on the mill floor, and on the threshold where the door hung on broken hinges. Peeping out, I saw that between me and the dovecot was a piece of bare cobbled ground, where no footmarks would show. Also it was mercifully hid by the mill buildings from any view from the house. I slipped across the space, got to the back of the dovecot and prospected a way of ascent.

2 **palsy:** Lähmung.
5 **please God:** so Gott will.
12 **dovecot:** (turmartiger) Taubenschlag.
20 **hinge:** (Tür-)Angel.
21 **cobbled:** gepflastert.
25 **to prospect:** erforschen, erkunden, untersuchen.
ascent: Aufstieg, Aufgang.

That was one of the hardest jobs I ever took on. My shoulder and arm ached like hell, and I was so sick and giddy that I was always on the verge of falling. But I managed it somehow. By the use of out-jutting stones and gaps in the masonry and a tough ivy root I got to the top in the end. There was a little parapet behind which I found space to lie down. Then I proceeded to go off into an old-fashioned swoon.

I woke with a burning head and the sun glaring in my face. For a long time I lay motionless, for those horrible fumes seemed to have loosened my joints and dulled my brain. Sounds came to me from the house – men speaking throatily and the throbbing of a stationary car. There was a little gap in the parapet to which I wriggled, and from which I had some sort of prospect of the yard. I saw figures come out – a servant with his head bound up, and then a younger man in knickerbockers. They were looking for something, and moved towards the mill. Then one of them caught sight of the wisp of cloth on the nail, and cried out to the other. They both

3 **giddy:** schwindelig.
4 **out-jutting:** vorspringend, hervorragend.
5 **masonry:** Mauerwerk.
6 **parapet:** Brüstung.
8 **swoon:** Ohnmacht(sanfall).
9 f. **sun glaring in my face:** Die Taubenschlagszene ist eine literarische Verbeugung vor Robert Louis Stevensons Abenteuerroman *Kidnapped* (1886), in welchem die beiden Helden auf einem Felsen festsitzen, während unten Truppen nach ihnen suchen (*to glare:* leuchten, strahlen).
13 **throatily** (adv.): kehlig, rauh, heiser.
throbbing: Pochen, Klopfen, Hämmern.
stationary: (still)stehend.

went back to the house, and brought two more to look at it. I saw the rotund figure of my late captor, and I thought I made out the man with the lisp. I noticed that all had pistols.

For half an hour they ransacked the mill. I could hear them kicking over the barrels and pulling up the rotten planking. Then they came outside, and stood just below the dovecot, arguing fiercely. The servant with the bandage was being soundly rated. I heard them fiddling with the door of the dovecot, and for one horrid moment I fancied they were coming up. Then they thought better of it, and went back to the house.

All that long blistering afternoon I lay baking on the rooftop. Thirst was my chief torment. My tongue was like a stick, and to make it worse I could hear the cool drip of water from the mill-lade. I watched the course of the little stream as it came in from the moor, and my fancy followed it to the top of the glen, where it must issue from an icy fountain fringed with cool ferns and mosses. I would have given a thousand pounds to plunge my face into that.

I had a fine prospect of the whole ring of moorland. I saw the car speed away with two occupants, and a man on a hill pony riding east. I judged they were looking for me, and I wished them joy of their quest.

2 **rotund:** rundlich.
my late captor: der mich zuletzt gefangennahm.
3 **lisp:** Lispeln.
9 f. **to fiddle with s.th.:** an etwas herumfingern.
19 **to fringe:** säumen, einfassen.
fern: Farnkraut.
21 **to plunge:** tauchen.

But I saw something else more interesting. The house stood almost on the summit of a swell of moorland which crowned a sort of plateau, and there was no higher point nearer than the big hills six miles off. The actual summit, as I have mentioned, was a biggish clump of trees – firs mostly, with a few ashes and beeches. On the dovecot I was almost on a level with the tree-tops, and could see what lay beyond. The wood was not solid, but only a ring, and inside was an oval of green turf, for all the world like a big cricket-field.

I didn't take long to guess what it was. It was an aerodrome, and a secret one. The place had been most cunningly chosen. For suppose anyone were watching an aeroplane descending here, he would think it had gone over the hill beyond the trees. As the place was on the top of a rise in the midst of a big amphitheatre, any observer from any direction would conclude it had passed out of view behind the hill. Only a man very close at hand would realize that the aeroplane had not gone over but had descended in the midst of the wood. An observer with a telescope on one of the higher hills might have discovered the truth, but only herds went there, and herds do not carry spy-glasses. When I looked from the dovecot I could see far away a blue line which I knew was the sea, and I grew furious to

6 **clump:** (Baum-)Gruppe.
ash: Esche.
7 **beech:** Buche.
12 f. **aerodrome:** Flugplatz.
13 f. **cunningly** (adv.): klug, schlau, geschickt.

think that our enemies had this secret conning-tower to rake our waterways.

Then I reflected that if that aeroplane came back the chances were ten to one that I would be discovered. So through the afternoon I lay and prayed for the coming of darkness, and glad I was when the sun went down over the big western hills and the twilight haze crept over the moor. The aeroplane was late. The gloaming was far advanced when I heard the beat of wings and saw it vol-planing downward to its home in the wood. Lights twinkled for a bit and there was much coming and going from the house. Then the dark fell and silence.

Thank God it was black night. The moon was well on its last quarter and would not rise till late. My thirst was too great to allow me to tarry, so about nine o'clock, so far as I could judge, I started to descend. It wasn't easy, and half-way down I heard the back door of the house open, and saw the gleam of a lantern against the mill wall. For some agonizing minutes I hung by the ivy and prayed that whoever it was would not come round by the dovecot. Then the light disappeared, and I dropped as softly as I could on to the hard soil of the yard.

I crawled on my belly in the lee of a stone dyke till I reached the fringe of trees which surrounded the house. If I had known how to do it I would have tried to put that aeroplane out of action, but I realized that

1 **conning-tower:** Kommandoturm.
2 **to rake:** absuchen.
7 **haze:** Dunst.
10 **to vol-plane:** einen Gleitflug machen, im Gleitflug niedergehen.
16 **to tarry:** zögern, zaudern; verweilen, bleiben.

any attempt would probably be futile. I was pretty certain that there would be some kind of defence round the house, so I went through the wood on hands and knees, feeling carefully every inch before me. It was as well, for presently I came on a wire about two feet from the ground. If I had tripped over that, it would doubtless have rung some bell in the house and I would have been captured.

A hundred yards farther on I found another wire cunningly placed on the edge of a small stream. Beyond that lay the moor, and in five minutes I was deep in bracken and heather. Soon I was round the shoulder of the rise, in the little glen from which the mill-lade flowed. Ten minutes later my face was in the spring, and I was soaking down pints of the blessed water.

But I did not stop till I had put half a dozen miles between me and that accursed dwelling.

Chapter VII

The Dry-Fly Fisherman

I sat down on a hill-top and took stock of my position. I wasn't feeling very happy, for my natural thankfulness at my escape was clouded by my severe bodily discom-

1 **futile:** nutzlos, sinnlos, zwecklos, vergeblich, aussichtslos.
6 **to trip:** stolpern, straucheln.
17 **accursed:** verflucht, unselig, verflixt.
19 **dry-fly:** Trockenfliege (Angeln).

fort. Those lentonite fumes had fairly poisoned me, and the baking hours on the dovecot hadn't helped matters. I had a crushing headache, and felt as sick as a cat. Also my shoulder was in a bad way. At first I thought it was only a bruise, but it seemed to be swelling, and I had no use of my left arm.

My plan was to seek Mr Turnbull's cottage, recover my garments, and especially Scudder's note-book, and then make for the main line and get back to the south. It seemed to me that the sooner I got in touch with the Foreign Office man, Sir Walter Bullivant, the better. I didn't see how I could get more proof than I had got already. He must just take or leave my story, and anyway, with him I would be in better hands than those devilish Germans. I had begun to feel quite kindly towards the British police.

It was a wonderful starry night, and I had not much difficulty about the road. Sir Harry's map had given me the lie of the land, and all I had to do was to steer a point or two west of south-west to come to the stream where I had met the roadman. In all these travels I never knew the names of the places, but I believe this stream was no less than the upper waters of the River Tweed. I calculated I must be about eighteen miles distant, and that meant I could not get there before morning. So I must lie up a day somewhere, for I was too outrageous a figure to be seen in the sunlight. I had neither coat, waistcoat, collar, nor hat, my trousers were badly torn, and my face and hands were black with the explosion. I daresay I had other beauties, for my eyes

27 **outrageous:** ungeheuerlich, schändlich, empörend.

felt as if they were furiously bloodshot. Altogether I was no spectacle for God-fearing citizens to see on a highroad.

Very soon after daybreak I made an attempt to clean myself in a hill burn, and then approached a herd's cottage, for I was feeling the need of food. He was away from home, and his wife was alone, with no neighbour for five miles. She was a decent old body, and a plucky one, for though she got a fright when she saw me, she had an axe handy, and would have used it on any evildoer. I told her that I had had a fall – I didn't say how – and she saw by my looks that I was pretty sick. Like a true Samaritan she asked no questions, but gave me a bowl of milk with a dash of whisky in it, and let me sit for a little by her kitchen fire. She would have bathed my shoulder, but it ached so badly that I would not let her touch it.

I don't know what she took me for – a repentant burglar, perhaps; for when I wanted to pay her for the milk and tendered a sovereign, which was the smallest coin I had, she shook her head and said something about "giving it to them that had a right to it". At this I protested so strongly that I think she believed me honest, for she took the money and gave me a warm new plaid for it, and an old hat of her man's. She showed me how to wrap the plaid round my shoulders, and when I left

1 **bloodshot:** blutunterlaufen.
2 **spectacle:** Anblick.
8 **body** (infml.): Mensch, Person.
plucky: mutig.
18 **repentant:** reuig, bußfertig.
20 **to tender:** anbieten, bereithalten.

that cottage I was the living image of the kind of Scotsman you see in the illustrations to Burns's poems. But at any rate I was more or less clad.

It was as well, for the weather changed before midday to a thick drizzle of rain. I found shelter below an overhanging rock in the crook of a burn, where a drift of dead brackens made a tolerable bed. There I managed to sleep till nightfall, waking very cramped and wretched, with my shoulder gnawing like a toothache. I ate the oakcake and cheese the old wife had given me and set out again just before the darkening.

I pass over the miseries of that night among the wet hills. There were no stars to steer by, and I had to do the best I could from my memory of the map. Twice I lost my way, and I had some nasty falls into peatbogs. I had only about ten miles to go as the crow flies, but my mistakes made it nearer twenty. The last bit was completed with set teeth and a very light and dizzy head. But I managed it, and in the early dawn I was knocking at Mr Turnbull's door. The mist lay close and thick, and from the cottage I could not see the highroad.

Mr Turnbull himself opened to me – sober and some-

2 **Burns:** Robert B. (1759–96), berühmtester Dichter Schottlands.
3 **clad:** Part. Perf. von *to clothe:* (be-, ein)kleiden.
5 **drizzle:** Nieselregen.
6 **crook:** Krümmung, Biegung.
7 **drift:** zusammengewehter Haufen.
8 **cramped:** gelähmt.
15 **peatbog:** Torfmoor.
16 **as the crow flies:** schnurgerade, Luftlinie.
18 **dizzy:** schwindelig.

thing more than sober. He was primly dressed in an ancient but well-tended suit of black; he had been shaved not later than the night before; he wore a linen collar; and in his left hand he carried a pocket Bible. At first he did not recognize me.

"Whae are ye that comes stravaigin' here on the Sabbath mornin'?" he asked.

I had lost all count of the days. So the Sabbath was the reason for this strange decorum.

My head was swimming so wildly that I could not frame a coherent answer. But he recognized me, and he saw that I was ill.

"Hae ye got my specs?" he asked.

I fetched them out of my trouser pocket and gave him them.

"Ye'll have come for your jaicket and westcoat," he said. "Come in-bye. Losh, man, ye're terrible dune i' the legs. Haud up till I get ye to a chair."

I perceived I was in for a bout of malaria. I had a good deal of fever in my bones, and the wet night had brought it out, while my shoulder and the effects of the fumes combined to make me feel pretty bad. Before I knew, Mr Turnbull was helping me off with my clothes, and putting me to bed in one of the two cupboards that lined the kitchen walls.

1 **primly** (adv.): steif, formell, gekünstelt.
6 **to come stravaigin':** etwa: ziellos herumwandern.
9 **decorum:** hier: Ausstaffierung.
11 **coherent:** zusammenhängend.
13 **specs:** Kurzform von *spectacles.*
17 **losh:** Ausruf; etwa: oh!, ah!
19 **bout:** (Krankheits-)Anfall, Attacke.

He was a true friend in need, that old roadman. His wife was dead years ago, and since his daughter's marriage he lived alone.

For the better part of ten days he did all the rough nursing I needed. I simply wanted to be left in peace while the fever took its course, and when my skin was cool again I found that the bout had more or less cured my shoulder. But it was a baddish go, and though I was out of bed in five days, it took me some time to get my legs again.

He went out each morning, leaving me milk for the day, and locking the door behind him; and came in in the evening to sit silent in the chimney corner. Not a soul came near the place. When I was getting better, he never bothered me with a question. Several times he fetched me a two days' old *Scotsman*, and I noticed that the interest in the Portland Place murder seemed to have died down. There was no mention of it, and I could find very little about anything except a thing called the General Assembly – some ecclesiastical spree, I gathered.

One day he produced my belt from a lockfast drawer. "There's a terrible heap o' siller in't," he said. "Ye'd better coont it to see it's a' there."

He never even sought my name. I asked him if anybody had been around making inquiries subsequent to my spell at the roadmaking.

8 **baddish go:** ziemlich schlimme Sache.

20 **General Assembly:** jährlich einberufenes Parlament der Church of Scotland, das immer im Mai zusammentrifft. Buchan war 1933/34 sein Hochkommissar.

ecclesiastical: kirchlich, geistlich.

26 **subsequent:** nachfolgend.

"Ay, there was a man in a motor-cawr. He speired whae had ta'en my place that day, and I let on I thocht him daft. But he keepit on at me, and syne I said he maun be thinkin' o' my gude-brither frae the Cleuch that whiles lent me a haun'. He was a wersh-lookin' sowl, and I couldna understand the half o' his English tongue."

I was getting restless those last days, and as soon as I felt myself fit I decided to be off. That was not till the twelfth day of June, and as luck would have it a drover went past that morning taking some cattle to Moffat. He was a man named Hislop, a friend of Turnbull's, and he came in to his breakfast with us and offered to take me with him.

I made Turnbull accept five pounds for my lodging, and a hard job I had of it. There never was a more independent being. He grew positively rude when I pressed him, and shy and red, and took the money at last without a thank you. When I told him how much I owed him, he grunted something about "ae guid turn deservin' anither". You would have thought from our leave-taking that we had parted in disgust.

Hislop was a cheery soul, who chattered all the way over the pass and down the sunny vale of Annan. I

3 **syne** (Scot.): schließlich.
4 **gude-brither** (Scot.): Schwager.
Cleuch (Scot.): wörtl.: Hügel; vermutl. fiktiver Name oder Abkürzung für einen existenten Ort.
5 **wersh-lookin'** (Scot.): rauhbeinig, mit harten, rauhen Zügen.
10 **drover:** Viehtreiber(in).
11 **Moffat:** Stadt in Schottland.
24 **Annan:** Fluß in Dumfries and Galloway.

talked of Galloway markets and sheep prices, and he made up his mind I was a "pack-shepherd" from those parts – whatever that may be. My plaid and my old hat, as I have said, gave me a fine theatrical Scots look. But driving cattle is a mortally slow job, and we took the better part of the day to cover a dozen miles.

If I had not had such an anxious heart I would have enjoyed that time. It was shining blue weather, with a constantly changing prospect of brown hills and far green meadows, and a continual sound of larks and curlews and falling streams. But I had no mind for the summer, and little for Hislop's conversation, for as the fateful fifteenth of June drew near I was overweighed with the hopeless difficulties of my enterprise.

I got some dinner in a humble Moffat public-house, and walked the two miles to the junction on the main line. The night express for the south was not due till near midnight, and to fill up the time I went up on the hillside and fell asleep, for the walk had tired me. I all but slept too long, and had to run to the station and catch the train with two minutes to spare. The feel of the hard third-class cushions and the smell of stale tobacco cheered me up wonderfully. At any rate, I felt now that I was getting to grips with my job.

2 **pack-shepherd:** Schaftreiber(in).
10 **lark:** Lerche.
16 **junction:** Knotenpunkt, Verbindungsstelle; Einmündung.
23 **stale:** alt, schal, schlecht, verdorben.
24 **to get to grips with s.th.:** etwas in den Griff bekommen.

I was decanted at Crewe in the small hours and had to wait till six to get a train for Birmingham. In the afternoon I got to Reading, and changed into a local train which journeyed into the deeps of Berkshire. Presently I was in a land of lush water-meadows and slow reedy streams. About eight o'clock in the evening, a weary and travel-stained being – a cross between a farm-labourer and a vet – with a checked black-and-white plaid over his arm (for I did not dare to wear it south of the Border), decended at the little station of Artinswell. There were several people on the platform, and I thought I had better wait to ask my way till I was clear of the place.

The road led through a wood of great beeches and then into a shallow valley, with the green backs of downs peeping over the distant trees. After Scotland the air smelt heavy and flat, but infinitely sweet, for the limes and chestnuts and lilac bushes were domes of blossom. Presently I came to a bridge, below which a clear slow stream flowed between snowy beds of water-buttercups. A little above it was a mill; and the lasher made

1 **to decant s.o.:** (fig.) jdn. abladen.
Crewe: Eisenbahnknotenpunkt in der mittelenglischen Grafschaft Cheshire.
the small hours: die frühen Morgenstunden.
5 **lush:** saftig, üppig.
reedy: schilfreich, schilfbewachsen.
15 **downs** (pl.): waldloses, grasbewachsenes Hügelland.
17 **lime:** Linde.
18 **chestnut:** Kastanie(nbaum).
lilac: Flieder.
dome: Kuppel.
21 **lasher:** Wehr.

a pleasant cool sound in the scented dusk. Somehow the place soothed me and put me at my ease. I fell to whistling as I looked into the green depths, and the tune which came to my lips was “Annie Laurie”. A fisherman came up from the waterside, and as he neared me he too began to whistle. The tune was infectious, for he followed my suit. He was a huge man in untidy old flannels and a wide-brimmed hat, with a canvas bag slung on his shoulder. He nodded to me, and I thought I had never seen a shrewder or better-tempered face. He leaned his delicate ten-foot split-cane rod against the bridge, and looked with me at the water.

“Clear, isn’t it?” he said pleasantly. “I back our Kennet any day against the Test. Look at that big fellow. Four pounds if he’s an ounce. But the evening rise is over and you can’t tempt ’em.”

“I don’t see him,” said I.

“Look! There! A yard from the reeds just above that stickle.”

“I’ve got him now. You might swear he was a black stone.”

8 **wide-brimmed:** breitkrempig.
9 **canvas:** Segeltuch.
11 f. **split-cane rod:** sechseckige, flexible Angelrute, aus gespaltenen, dreieckigen, seitlich abgeflachten Bambusrohrstreifen kunstvoll zusammengefügt und verleimt.
15 **Test:** Fluß in der südenglischen Grafschaft Hampshire.
16 **pound:** Gewichtseinheit; 1 pound entspricht 453,59 g.
ounce: Unze, Gewichtseinheit; 1 ounce entspricht 28,35 g.
19 **reed:** Ried, Schilf(rohr).
20 **stickle:** kleiner Zweig.

"So," he said, and whistled another bar of "Annie Laurie".

"Twisdon's the name, isn't it?" he said over his shoulder, his eyes still fixed on the stream.

"No," I said. "I mean to say, Yes." I had forgotten all about my alias.

"It's a wise conspirator that knows his own name," he observed, grinning broadly at a moor-hen that emerged from the bridge's shadow.

I stood up and looked at him, at the square, cleft jaw and broad, lined brow and the firm folds of cheek, and began to think that here at last was an ally worth having. His whimsical blue eyes seemed to go very deep.

Suddenly he frowned. "I call it disgraceful," he said, raising his voice. "Disgraceful that an able-bodied man like you should dare to beg. You can get a meal from my kitchen, but you'll get no money from me."

A dog-cart was passing, driven by a young man who raised his whip to salute the fisherman. When he had gone, he picked up his rod.

"That's my house," he said, pointing to a white gate a hundred yards on. "Wait five minutes and then go round to the back door." And with that he left me.

I did as I was bidden. I found a pretty cottage with a

6 **alias:** falscher Name.
7 **conspirator:** Verschwörer(in).
8 **moor-hen:** gemeines Teichhuhn, weibliches Moorhuhn.
10 **cleft jaw:** gespaltenes Kinn, Kinn mit Grube.
13 **whimsical:** humorig, launig, wunderlich, seltsam.
15 **disgraceful:** skandalös, eine Schande.
19 **dog-cart:** zweirädriger Einspänner.

lawn running down to the stream, and a perfect jungle of guelder-rose and lilac flanking the path. The back door stood open, and a grave butler was awaiting me. "Come this way, sir," he said, and he led me along a passage and up a back staircase to a pleasant bedroom looking towards the river. There I found a complete outfit laid out for me – dress clothes with all the fixings, a brown flannel suit, shirts, collars, ties, shaving things, and hair-brushes, even a pair of patent shoes. "Sir Walter thought as how Mr Reggie's things would fit you, sir," said the butler. "He keeps some clothes 'ere, for he comes regular on the week-ends. There's a bathroom next door, and I've prepared a 'ot bath. Dinner in 'alf an hour, sir. You'll 'ear the gong."

The grave being withdrew, and I sat down in a chintz-covered easy-chair and gaped. It was like a pantomime, to come suddenly out of beggardom into this orderly comfort. Obviously Sir Walter believed in me, though why he did I could not guess. I looked at myself in the mirror and saw a wild, haggard brown fellow, with a fortnight's ragged beard, and dust in ears and eyes, collarless, vulgarly shirted, with shapeless old tweed clothes and boots that had not been cleaned for the better part of a month. I made a fine tramp and a fair drover; and here I was ushered by a prim butler into

1 **jungle:** Dschungel.
2 **guelder-rose:** Schneeball (Busch).
7 **fixings** (pl.): Zubehör; (fig.) Drum und Dran.
15 f. **chintz-covered:** mit Chintzbezug.
16 **easy-chair:** Sessel.
to gape: erstaunt starren.
20 **haggard:** ausgezehrt, abgehärmt; abgespannt.

this temple of gracious ease. And the best of it was that they did not even know my name.

I resolved not to puzzle my head but to take the gifts the gods had provided. I shaved and bathed luxuriously, and got into the dress clothes and clean crackling shirt, which fitted me not so badly. By the time I had finished the looking-glass showed a not unpersonable young man.

Sir Walter awaited me in a dusky dining-room where a little round table was lit with silver candles. The sight of him – so respectable and established and secure, the embodiment of law and government and all the conventions – took me aback and made me feel an interloper. He couldn't know the truth about me, or he wouldn't treat me like this. I simply could not accept his hospitality on false pretences.

"I'm more obliged to you than I can say, but I'm bound to make things clear," I said. "I'm an innocent man, but I'm wanted by the police. I've got to tell you this, and I won't be surprised if you kick me out."

He smiled. "That's all right. Don't let that interfere with your appetite. We can talk about these things after dinner."

I never ate a meal with greater relish, for I had had nothing all day but railway sandwiches. Sir Walter did me proud, for we drank a good champagne and had some uncommon fine port afterwards. It made me al-

12 **embodiment:** Verkörperung.
13 **to take s.o. aback:** jdn. verblüffen.
13 f. **interloper:** Eindringling.
25 f. **to do s.o. proud** (infml.): jdm. große Ehre erweisen; jdn. königlich bewirten.

most hysterical to be sitting there, waited on by a footman and a sleek butler, and remember that I had been living for three weeks like a brigand, with every man's hand against me. I told Sir Walter about tiger-fish in the Zambesi that bite off your fingers if you give them a chance, and we discussed sport up and down the globe, for he had hunted a bit in his day.

We went to his study for coffee, a jolly room full of books and trophies and untidiness and comfort. I made up my mind that if ever I got rid of this business and had a house of my own, I would create just such a room. Then when the coffee-cups were cleared away, and we had got our cigars alight, my host swung his long legs over the side of his chair and bade me get started with my yarn.

"I've obeyed Harry's instructions," he said, "and the bribe he offered me was that you would tell me something to wake me up. I'm ready, Mr Hannay."

I noticed with a start that he called me by my proper name.

I began at the very beginning. I told of my boredom in London, and the night I had come back to find Scudder gibbering on my doorstep. I told him all Scudder had told me about Karolides and the Foreign Office conference, and that made him purse his lips and grin.

3 **brigand:** Bandit, (Straßen-)Räuber.
4 **tiger-fish:** Tigersalmler (mit dem südamerikanischen Piranha verwandter gestreifter Raubfisch in den großen Flüssen Afrikas).
5 **Zambesi:** Sambesi, Fluß in Afrika.
17 **bribe:** Bestechung(sgeld, -sgeschenk).
23 **to gibber:** schnattern, quatschen.
25 **to purse one's lips:** die Lippen schürzen, kräuseln, den Mund verziehen.

Then I got to the murder, and he grew solemn again. He heard all about the milkman and my time in Galloway, and my deciphering Scudder's notes at the inn.

"You've got them here?" he asked sharply, and drew a long breath when I whipped the little book from my pocket.

I said nothing of the contents. Then I described my meeting with Sir Harry, and the speeches at the hall. At that he laughed uproariously.

"Harry talked dashed nonsense, did he? I quite believe it. He's as good a chap as ever breathed, but his idiot of an uncle has stuffed his head with maggots. Go on, Mr Hannay."

My day as roadman excited him a bit. He made me describe the two fellows in the car very closely, and seemed to be raking back in his memory. He grew merry again when he heard of the fate of that ass Jopley.

But the old man in the moorland house solemnized him. Again I had to describe every detail of his appearance.

"Bland and bald-headed and hooded his eyes like a bird. . . . He sounds a sinister wild-fowl! And you dynamited his hermitage, after he had saved you from the police. Spirited piece of work, that!"

9 **uproariously** (adv.): schallend, laut.
10 **dashed** (infml.): verflixt.
12 **maggot** (fig.): Grille, verrückte Idee.
19 **to solemnize:** feiern, feierlich nennen.
22 **bland:** mild, sanft, höflich, verbindlich; (ein)schmeichelnd; kühl.
23 **sinister:** finster, unheimlich, böse.
wild-fowl: Wildvogel.
25 **spirited:** beherzt, mutig.

Presently I reached the end of my wanderings. He got up slowly, and looked down at me from the hearth-rug.

"You may dismiss the police from your mind," he said. "You're in no danger from the law of this land."

"Great Scot!" I cried. "Have they got the murderer?"

"No. But for the last fortnight they have dropped you from the list of possibles."

"Why?" I asked in amazement.

"Principally because I received a letter from Scudder. I knew something of the man, and he did several jobs for me. He was half crank, half genius, but he was wholly honest. The trouble about him was his partiality for playing a lone hand. That made him pretty well useless in any Secret Service – a pity, for he had uncommon gifts. I think he was the bravest man in the world, for he was always shivering with fright, and yet nothing would choke him off. I had a letter from him on the 31st of May."

"But he had been dead a week by then."

"The letter was written and posted on the 23rd. He evidently did not anticipate an immediate decease. His communications usually took a week to reach me, for they were sent under cover to Spain and then to Newcastle. He had a mania, you know, for concealing his tracks."

5 **Great Scot!:** Ausruf; etwa: ach du meine Güte!, ach du lieber Gott!
12 **crank:** Spinner(in), harmlose(r) Verrückte(r).
13 **partiality:** Vorliebe.
18 **to choke s.o. off** (infml.): jdn. abwimmeln, abwürgen.
22 **decease:** Ableben.
25 **to have a mania for doing s.th.:** etwas leidenschaftlich gern tun.

"What did he say?" I stammered.

"Nothing. Merely that he was in danger, but had found shelter with a good friend, and that I would hear from him before the 15th of June. He gave me no address, but said he was living near Portland Place. I think his object was to clear you if anything happened. When I got it I went to Scotland Yard, went over the details of the inquest, and concluded that you were the friend. We made inquiries about you, Mr Hannay, and found you were respectable. I thought I knew the motives for your disappearance – not only the police, the other one too – and when I got Harry's scrawl I guessed at the rest. I have been expecting you any time this past week."

You can imagine what a load this took off my mind. I felt a free man once more, for I was now up against my country's enemies only, and not my country's law.

"Now let us have the little note-book," said Sir Walter.

It took us a good hour to work through it. I explained the cypher, and he was jolly quick at picking it up. He emended my reading of it on several points, but I had been fairly correct, on the whole. His face was very grave before he had finished, and he sat silent for a while.

"I don't know what to make of it," he said at last. "He is right about one thing – what is going to happen the day after to-morrow. How the devil can it have got known? That is ugly enough in itself. But all this about war and the Black Stone – it reads like some wild melo-

12 **scrawl:** Gekritzel, Geschreibsel.
21 **to emend:** verbessern, korrigieren.

drama. If only I had more confidence in Scudder's judgement. The trouble about him was that he was too romantic. He had the artistic temperament, and wanted a story to be better than God meant it to be. He had a lot of odd biases, too. Jews, for example, made him see red. Jews and the high finance.

The Black Stone," he repeated. "*Der Schwarzestein*. It's like a penny novelette. And all this stuff about Karolides. That is the weak part of the tale, for I happen to know that the virtuous Karolides is likely to outlast us both. There is no State in Europe that wants him gone. Besides, he has just been playing up to Berlin and Vienna and giving my Chief some uneasy moments. No! Scudder has gone off the track there. Frankly, Hannay, I don't believe that part of his story. There's some nasty business afoot, and he found out too much and lost his life over it. But I am ready to take my oath that it is ordinary spy work. A certain great European Power makes a hobby of her spy system, and her methods are not too particular. Since she pays by piecework her blackguards are not likely to stick at a murder or two. They want our naval dispositions for their collection at the Marineamt; but they will be pigeon-holed – nothing more."

5 **bias:** Vorurteil, Voreingenommenheit.
8 **penny novelette:** Groschenroman.
12 **to play up to s.o.:** jdm. schöntun, sich bei jdm. beliebt machen.
16 **afoot:** (fig.) im Gange, Anzug, Kommen.
17 **to take an oath:** einen Eid leisten, schwören.
20 **piecework:** Akkordarbeit.
21 **blackguard:** Lump, Schuft.
23 **to pigeon-hole s.th.:** etwas in die Schublade wandern lassen, auf Eis legen.

Just then the butler entered the room.

"There's a trunk-call from London, Sir Walter. It's Mr 'Eath, and he wants to speak to you personally."

My host went off to the telephone.

He returned in five minutes with a whitish face. "I apologize to the shade of Scudder," he said. "Karolides was shot dead this evening at a few minutes after seven."

Chapter VIII

The Coming of the Black Stone

I came down to breakfast next morning, after eight hours of blessed dreamless sleep, to find Sir Walter decoding a telegram in the midst of muffins and marmalade. His fresh rosiness of yesterday seemed a thought tarnished.

"I had a busy hour on the telephone after you went to bed," he said. "I got my Chief to speak to the First Lord and the Secretary for War, and they are bringing Royer over a day sooner. This wire clinches it. He will

2 **trunk-call:** Ferngespräch.
13 **muffin:** Hefeteigsemmel.
15 **tarnished:** getrübt, glanzlos, stumpf.
17 f. **First Lord:** politischer Oberbefehlshaber der Admiralität; vermutl. Anspielung auf Winston Churchill (1874–1965), den späteren Premierminister und Führer der konservativen Partei.
18 **Secretary for War:** Kriegsminister.
19 **this clinches it:** hiermit ist die Sache entschieden, damit ist der Fall klar.

be in London at five. Odd that the code word for a *Sous-chef d'État Major-Général* should be 'Porker'."

He directed me to the hot dishes and went on.

"Not that I think it will do much good. If your friends were clever enough to find out the first arrangement they are clever enough to discover the change. I would give my head to know where the leak is. We believed there were only five men in England who knew about Royer's visit, and you may be certain there were fewer in France, for they manage these things better there."

While I ate he continued to talk, making me to my surprise a present of his full confidence.

"Can the dispositions not be changed?" I asked.

"They could," he said. "But we want to avoid that if possible. They are the result of immense thought, and no alteration would be as good. Besides, on one or two points change is simply impossible. Still, something could be done, I suppose, if it were absolutely necessary. But you see the difficulty, Hannay. Our enemies are not going to be such fools as to pick Royer's pocket or any childish game like that. They know that would mean a row and put us on our guard. Their aim is to get the details without any one of us knowing, so that Royer will go back to Paris in the belief that the whole business is still deadly secret. If they can't do that they

2 **Sous-chef d'État Major-Général** (Fr.): zweiter Generalstabschef. **Porker:** sprechender Name; wörtl.: Mastschwein.

7 **leak:** Leck, undichte Stelle.

10 f. **they manage these things better there:** Anspielung auf die einleitende Zeile von Laurence Sternes Reisebuch *A Sentimental Journey* (1768) und damit ein Beleg für Sir Walters Bildung.

fail, for, once we suspect, they know that the whole thing must be altered."

"Then we must stick by the Frenchman's side till he is home again," I said. "If they thought they could get the information in Paris they would try there. It means that they have some deep scheme on foot in London which they reckon is going to win out."

"Royer dines with my Chief, and then comes to my house where four people will see him – Whittaker from the Admiralty, myself, Sir Arthur Drew, and General Winstanley. The First Lord is ill, and has gone to Sheringham. At my house he will get a certain document from Whittaker, and after that he will be motored to Portsmouth where a destroyer will take him to Havre. His journey is too important for the ordinary boat-train. He will never be left unattended for a moment till he is safe on French soil. The same with Whittaker till he meets Royer. That is the best we can do, and it's hard to see how there can be any miscarriage. But I don't mind admitting that I'm horribly nervous. This murder of Karolides will play the deuce in the chancelleries of Europe."

6 **on foot:** (fig.) im Gange.
7 **to win out** (infml.): sich durchsetzen.
11 **The First Lord is ill:** Winston Churchill wurde vom 25. bis 27. Juli 1914 tatsächlich durch die Krankheit seiner Frau in dem ostenglischen Seebad Cromer in der Grafschaft Norfolk aufgehalten.
11 f. **Sheringham:** Seebad direkt westlich von Cromer.
14 **Havre:** Le Havre, nordfranzösische Hafenstadt.
19 **miscarriage:** Fehlschlag(en), Mißlingen.
21 **to play the deuce** (infml.): einen Wirbel verursachen, Schindluder treiben.
21 f. **chancellery:** Botschaft, Konsulat.

After breakfast he asked me if I could drive a car.

"Well, you'll be my chauffeur to-day and wear Hudson's rig. You're about his size. You have a hand in this business and we are taking no risks. There are desperate men against us, who will not respect the country retreat of an overworked official."

When I first came to London I had bought a car and amused myself with running about the south of England, so I knew something of the geography. I took Sir Walter to town by the Bath Road and made good going. It was a soft breathless June morning, with a promise of sultriness later, but it was delicious enough swinging through the little towns with their freshly watered streets, and past the summer gardens of the Thames valley. I landed Sir Walter at his house in Queen Anne's Gate punctually by half-past eleven. The butler was coming up by train with the luggage.

The first thing he did was to take me round to Scotland Yard. There we saw a prim gentleman, with a clean-shaven lawyer's face.

"I've brought you the Portland Place murderer," was Sir Walter's introduction.

The reply was a wry smile. "It would have been a welcome present, Bullivant. This, I presume, is Mr Richard Hannay, who for some days greatly interested my department."

12 **sultriness:** Schwüle.

15 f. **Queen Anne's Gate:** vornehmer Wohnbezirk zwischen St James's Park und Westminster im Zentrum Londons. Buchans Freund und Gönner Richard Burdon Haldane (1856–1928), Lordkanzler der Liberalen, jedoch Kriegsminister im Sommer 1914, wohnte hier und hielt am 3. August 1914 einen wichtigen Kriegsrat ab.

"Mr Hannay will interest it again. He has much to tell you, but not to-day. For certain grave reasons his tale must wait for twenty-four hours. Then, I can promise you, you will be entertained and possibly edified. I want you to assure Mr Hannay that he will suffer no further inconvenience."

This assurance was promptly given. "You can take up your life where you left off," I was told. "Your flat, which probably you no longer wish to occupy, is waiting for you, and your man is still there. As you were never publicly accused, we considered that there was no need of a public exculpation. But on that, of course, you must please yourself."

"We may want your assistance later on, MacGillivray," Sir Walter said as we left.

Then he turned me loose.

"Come and see me to-morrow, Hannay. I needn't tell you to keep deadly quiet. If I were you I would go to bed, for you must have considerable arrears of sleep to overtake. You had better lie low, for if one of your Black Stone friends saw you there might be trouble."

I felt curiously at a loose end. At first it was very pleasant to be a free man, able to go where I wanted without fearing anything. I had only been a month under the ban of the law, and it was quite enough for me. I went to the Savoy and ordered very carefully a very good

4 **to edify:** (fig.) erbauen, aufrichten.
12 **exculpation:** Entlastung.
19 **arrears** (pl.): Rückstand.
22 **to feel at a loose end:** nicht wissen, was man mit sich anfangen soll.
26 **Savoy:** Londoner Nobelhotel.

luncheon, and then smoked the best cigar the house could provide. But I was still feeling nervous. When I saw anybody look at me in the lounge, I grew shy, and wondered if they were thinking about the murder. After that I took a taxi and drove miles away up into North London. I walked back through fields and lines of villas and terraces and then slums and mean streets, and it took me pretty nearly two hours. All the while my restlessness was growing worse. I felt that great things, tremendous things, were happening or about to happen, and I, who was the cog-wheel of the whole business, was out of it. Royer would be landing at Dover, Sir Walter would be making plans with the few people in England who were in the secret, and somewhere in the darkness the Black Stone would be working. I felt the sense of danger and impending calamity, and I had the curious feeling, too, that I alone could avert it, alone could grapple with it. But I was out of the game now. How could it be otherwise? It was not likely that Cabinet Ministers and Admiralty Lords and Generals would admit me to their councils.

I actually began to wish that I could run up against one of my three enemies. That would lead to developments. I felt that I wanted enormously to have a vulgar scrap with those gentry, where I could hit out and flatten

11 **cog-wheel:** Zahnrad; (fig.) Triebkraft, Motor, Zentrum (des Geschehens).
16 **impending:** nahe bevorstehend, drohend.
calamity: Unheil, Katastrophe.
18 **to avert:** abwenden, abwehren, verhüten.
to grapple with s.th.: sich mit etwas auseinandersetzen.
20 **Admiralty Lord:** Vorsitzender der Admiralität.
24 **scrap** (slang): Keilerei, Prügelei.

something. I was rapidly getting into a very bad temper.

I didn't feel like going back to my flat. That had to be faced some time, but as I still had sufficient money I thought I would put it off till next morning, and go to a hotel for the night.

My irritation lasted through dinner, which I had at a restaurant in Jermyn Street. I was no longer hungry, and let several courses pass untasted. I drank the best part of a bottle of Burgundy, but it did nothing to cheer me. An abominable restlessness had taken possession of me. Here was I, a very ordinary fellow, with no particular brains, and yet I was convinced that somehow I was needed to help this business through – that without me it would all go to blazes. I told myself it was sheer silly conceit, that four or five of the cleverest people living, with all the might of the British Empire at their back, had the job in hand. Yet I couldn't be convinced. It seemed as if a voice kept speaking in my ear, telling me to be up and doing, or I would never sleep again.

The upshot was that about half-past nine I made up my mind to go to Queen Anne's Gate. Very likely I would not be admitted, but it would ease my conscience to try.

I walked down Jermyn Street, and at the corner of Duke Street passed a group of young men. They were in evening dress, had been dining somewhere, and were

8 **Jermyn Street:** Straße zwischen Piccadilly und St James's Park.
11 **abominable:** abscheulich, scheußlich.
16 **conceit:** Einbildung.
21 **upshot:** (End-)Ergebnis.
26 **Duke Street:** Straße zwischen Piccadilly und St James's Park.

going on to a music-hall. One of them was Mr Marmaduke Jopley.

He saw me and stopped short.

"By God, the murderer!" he cried. "Here, you fellows, hold him! That's Hannay, the man who did the Portland Place murder!" He gripped me by the arm, and the others crowded round.

I wasn't looking for any trouble, but my ill-temper made me play the fool. A policeman came up, and I should have told him the truth, and, if he didn't believe it, demanded to be taken to Scotland Yard, or for that matter to the nearest police station. But a delay at that moment seemed to me unendurable, and the sight of Marmie's imbecile face was more than I could bear. I let out with my left, and had the satisfaction of seeing him measure his length in the gutter.

Then began an unholy row. They were all on me at once, and the policeman took me in the rear. I got in one or two good blows, for I think, with fair play, I could have licked the lot of them, but the policeman pinned me behind, and one of them got his fingers on my throat.

Through a black cloud of rage I heard the officer of the law asking what was the matter, and Marmie, between his broken teeth, declaring that I was Hannay the murderer.

13 **unendurable:** unerträglich.
14 **imbecile:** idiotisch, dumm.
15 **to let out:** ausholen.
16 **gutter:** Rinnstein, Gosse.
18 **to take s.o. in the rear:** jdn. im Rücken fassen.
20 **to lick** (infml.): verdreschen, schlagen, besiegen.

"Oh, damn it all," I cried, "make the fellow shut up. I advise you to leave me alone, constable. Scotland Yard knows all about me, and you'll get a proper wigging if you interfere with me."

"You've got to come along of me, young man," said the policeman. "I saw you strike that gentleman crool 'ard. You began it too, for he wasn't doing nothing. I seen you. Best go quietly or I'll have to fix you up."

Exasperation and an overwhelming sense that at no cost must I delay gave me the strength of a bull elephant. I fairly wrenched the constable off his feet, floored the man who was gripping my collar, and set off at my best pace down Duke Street. I heard a whistle being blown, and the rush of men behind me.

I have a very fair turn of speed, and that night I had wings. In a jiffy I was in Pall Mall and had turned down towards St James's Park. I dodged the policeman at the Palace gates, dived through a press of carriages at the entrance to the Mall, and was making for the bridge before my pursuers had crossed the roadway. In the open ways of the Park I put on a spurt. Happily there were few people about and no one tried to

3 **wigging** (infml.): Standpauke.
4 **to interfere with s.o.:** jdn. stören, (be)hindern, belästigen.
6 **crool:** *cruel.*
8 **to fix s.o. up:** jdn. festnehmen.
9 **exasperation:** Wut.
16 **in a jiffy** (infml.): im Nu.
Pall Mall: Straße in der Nähe des St James's Park.
18 **Palace:** *Buckingham Palace.*
press: Gedränge.
19 **the Mall:** Prachtstraße zwischen Buckingham Palace und Trafalgar Square.

stop me. I was staking all on getting to Queen Anne's Gate.

When I entered that quiet thoroughfare it seemed deserted. Sir Walter's house was in the narrow part, and outside it three or four motor-cars were drawn up. I slackened speed some yards off and walked briskly up to the door. If the butler refused me admission, or if he even delayed to open the door, I was done.

He didn't delay. I had scarcely rung before the door opened.

"I must see Sir Walter," I panted. "My business is desperately important."

That butler was a great man. Without moving a muscle he held the door open, and then shut it behind me. "Sir Walter is engaged, sir, and I have orders to admit no one. Perhaps you will wait."

The house was of the old-fashioned kind, with a wide hall and rooms on both sides of it. At the far end was an alcove with a telephone and a couple of chairs, and there the butler offered me a seat.

"See here," I whispered. "There's trouble about and I'm in it. But Sir Walter knows, and I'm working for him. If anyone comes and asks if I am here, tell him a lie."

He nodded, and presently there was a noise of voices in the street, and a furious ringing at the bell. I never admired a man more than that butler. He opened the door, and with a face like a graven image waited to be

3 **thoroughfare:** Verkehrsader, Durchgangsstraße, Durchfahrt.
6 **briskly** (adv.): rasch.
19 **alcove:** Alkoven, Nische.
28 **graven image:** Götzenbild.

questioned. Then he gave them it. He told them whose house it was, and what his orders were, and simply froze them off the doorstep. I could see it all from my alcove, and it was better than any play.

I hadn't waited long till there came another ring at the bell. The butler made no bones about admitting this new visitor.

While he was taking off his coat I saw who it was. You couldn't open a newspaper or a magazine without seeing that face – the grey beard cut like a spade, the firm fighting mouth, the blunt square nose, and the keen blue eyes. I recognized the First Sea Lord, the man, they say, that made the new British Navy.

He passed my alcove and was ushered into a room at the back of the hall. As the door opened I could hear the sound of low voices. It shut, and I was left alone again.

For twenty minutes I sat there, wondering what I was to do next. I was still perfectly convinced that I was wanted, but when or how I had no notion. I kept looking at my watch, and as the time crept on to half-past ten I began to think that the conference must soon end. In a quarter of an hour Royer should be speeding along the road to Portsmouth. . . .

1 **he gave them it** (infml.): er hat es ihnen gegeben.
3 **to freeze s.o. off:** jdn. hinausekeln, kaltstellen.
6 **to make no bones:** nicht viel Federlesens machen, nicht lange fakkeln.
12 **First Sea Lord:** oberster Marinebefehlshaber der Admiralität; vermutl. Anspielung auf Admiral Prinz Ludwig Alexander von Battenberg (1854–1921), der tatsächlich einen Bart trug.

Then I heard a bell ring, and the butler appeared. The door of the back room opened, and the First Sea Lord came out. He walked past me, and in passing he glanced in my direction, and for a second we looked each other in the face.

Only for a second, but it was enough to make my heart jump. I had never seen the great man before, and he had never seen me. But in that fraction of time something sprang into his eyes, and that something was recognition. You can't mistake it. It is a flicker, a spark of light, a minute shade of difference which means one thing and one thing only. It came involuntarily, for in a moment it died, and he passed on. In a maze of wild fancies I heard the street door close behind him.

I picked up the telephone and looked up the number of his house. We were connected at once, and I heard a servant's voice.

"Is his Lordship at home?" I asked.

"His Lordship returned half an hour ago," said the voice, "and has gone to bed. He is not very well tonight. Will you leave a message, sir?"

I rang off and almost tumbled into a chair. My part in this business was not yet ended. It had been a close shave, but I had been in time.

Not a moment could be lost, so I marched boldly to the door of that back room and entered without knocking.

10 **flicker:** Funke, Anflug, Aufflackern.
12 **involuntarily** (adv.): unwillkürlich.
13 **maze:** Irrgarten, Labyrinth, Gewirr.
22 **to ring off:** (Hörer) auflegen.
23 f. **it had been a close shave** (infml.): das hätte ins Auge gehen können.

Five surprised faces looked up from a round table. There was Sir Walter, and Drew the War Minister, whom I knew from his photographs. There was a slim elderly man, who was probably Whittaker, the Admiralty offical, and there was General Winstanley, conspicuous from the long scar on his forehead. Lastly, there was a short stout man with an iron-grey moustache and bushy eyebrows, who had been arrested in the middle of a sentence.

Sir Walter's face showed surprise and annoyance.

"This is Mr Hannay, of whom I have spoken to you," he said apologetically to the company. "I'm afraid, Hannay, this visit is ill-timed."

I was getting back my coolness. "That remains to be seen, sir," I said; "but I think it may be in the nick of time. For God's sake, gentlemen, tell me who went out a minute ago?"

"Lord Alloa," Sir Walter said, reddening with anger.

"It was not," I cried, "it was his living image, but it was not Lord Alloa. It was someone who recognized me, someone I have seen in the last month. He had scarcely left the doorstep when I rang up Lord Alloa's house and was told he had come in half an hour before and had gone to bed."

"Who – who –" someone stammered.

"The Black Stone," I cried, and I sat down in the chair so recently vacated and looked round at five badly scared gentlemen.

15 f. **in the nick of time:** im richtigen Augenblick, im letzten Moment.
27 **to vacate:** räumen, frei machen.

Chapter IX

The Thirty-Nine Steps

"Nonsense!" said the official from the Admiralty.

Sir Walter got up and left the room while we looked blankly at the table. He came back in ten minutes with a long face. "I have spoken to Alloa," he said. "Had him out of bed – very grumpy. He went straight home after Mulross's dinner."

"But it's madness," broke in General Winstanley. "Do you mean to tell me that that man came here and sat beside me for the best part of half an hour and that I didn't detect the imposture? Alloa must be out of his mind."

"Don't you see the cleverness of it?" I said. "You were too interested in other things to have any eyes. You took Lord Alloa for granted. If it had been anybody else you might have looked more closely, but it was natural for him to be here, and that put you all to sleep."

Then the Frenchman spoke, very slowly, and in good English.

"The young man is right. His psychology is good. Our enemies have not been foolish!"

He bent his wise brows on the assembly.

"I will tell you a tale," he said. "It happened many

5 **blankly** (adv.): verdutzt, verlegen.
7 **grumpy:** mürrisch, mißmutig.
12 **imposture:** Betrug, Schwindel, Hochstapelei.

years ago in Senegal. I was quartered in a remote station, and to pass the time used to go fishing for big barbel in the river. A little Arab mare used to carry my luncheon-basket – one of the salted dun breed you got at Timbuctoo in the old days. Well, one morning I had good sport, and the mare was unaccountably restless. I could hear her whinnying and squealing and stamping her feet, and I kept soothing her with my voice while my mind was intent on fish. I could see her all the time, as I thought, out of a corner of my eye, tethered to a tree twenty yards away. After a couple of hours I began to think of food. I collected my fish in a tarpaulin bag, and moved down the stream towards the mare, trolling my line. When I got up to her I flung the tarpaulin on her back. . . ."

He paused and looked round.

"It was the smell that gave me warning. I turned my head and found myself looking at a lion three feet off. . . . An old man-eater, that was the terror of the village.

1 **Senegal:** Republik an der westafrikanischen Küste; ab 1895 Teil des Generalgouvernements Französisch-Westafrika.
to quarter: einquartieren.

2 f. **barbel:** Barbe (Fisch).

3 **mare:** Stute.

4 **salted** (slang): routiniert, erfahren.
dun: graubraun.

5 **Timbuctoo:** Timbuktu, Stadt an einer bedeutenden Karawanenstraße durch die Sahara in der afrikanischen Republik Mali; ab 1898 Teil von Französisch-Westafrika.

5 f. **to have good sport:** Vergnügen am Sport haben.

7 **to squeal:** aufschreien, quieken; (infml.) zetern, schimpfen.

12 **tarpaulin:** (geteertes) Segeltuch.

13 **to troll:** (Angel) schleppen.

... What was left of the mare, a mass of blood and bones and hide, was behind him."

"What happened?" I asked. I was enough of a hunter to know a true yarn when I heard it.

"I stuffed my fishing-rod into his jaws, and I had a pistol. Also my servants came presently with rifles. But he left his mark on me." He held up a hand which lacked three fingers.

"Consider," he said. "The mare had been dead more than an hour, and the brute had been patiently watching me ever since. I never saw the kill, for I was accustomed to the mare's fretting, and I never marked her absence, for my consciousness of her was only of something tawny, and the lion filled that part. If I could blunder thus, gentlemen, in a land where men's senses are keen, why should we busy preoccupied urban folk not err also?"

Sir Walter nodded. No one was ready to gainsay him.

"But I don't see," went on Winstanley. "Their object was to get these dispositions without our knowing it. Now it only required one of us to mention to Alloa our meeting to-night for the whole fraud to be exposed."

Sir Walter laughed dryly. "The selection of Alloa shows their acumen. Which of us was likely to speak to him

6 **rifle:** Gewehr (mit gezogenem Lauf), Büchse.
12 **fretting:** Unruhe.
14 **tawny:** lohfarben, gelbbraun.
15 **to blunder:** einen (groben) Fehler, einen Schnitzer machen, einen Bock schießen.
16 **preoccupied:** gedankenverloren.
18 **to gainsay s.o.:** jdm. widersprechen.
22 **fraud:** Schwindel, Betrug, arglistige Täuschung.
24 **acumen:** Scharfsinn.

about to-night? Or was he likely to open the subject?"

I remember the First Sea Lord's reputation for taciturnity and shortness of temper.

"The one thing that puzzles me," said the General, "is what good his visit here would do that spy fellow? He could not carry away several pages of figures and strange names in his head."

"That is not difficult," the Frenchman replied. "A good spy is trained to have a photographic memory. Like your own Macaulay. You noticed he said nothing, but went through these papers again and again. I think we may assume that he has every detail stamped on his mind. When I was younger I could do the same trick."

"Well, I suppose there is nothing for it but to change the plans," said Sir Walter ruefully.

Whittaker was looking very glum. "Did you tell Lord Alloa what has happened?" he asked. "No? Well, I can't speak with absolute assurance, but I'm nearly certain we can't make any serious change unless we alter the geography of England."

"Another thing must be said," it was Royer who spoke. "I talked freely when that man was here. I told something of the military plans of my Government. I was permitted to say so much. But that information would be worth many millions to our enemies. No, my friends,

3 f. **taciturnity:** Schweigsamkeit, Verschlossenheit.

11 **Macaulay:** Thomas Babington Lord M. (1800–59), anglo-schottischer Liberaler, Politiker, und Historiker; Großonkel von Buchans Freund, dem Historiker G. M. Trevelyan (1876–1962).

18 **glum:** verdrossen, bedrückt, niedergeschlagen.

I see no other way. The man who came here and his confederates must be taken, and taken at once."

"Good God," I cried, "and we have not a rag of a clue."

"Besides," said Whittaker, "there is the post. By this time the news will be on its way."

"No," said the Frenchman. "You do not understand the habits of the spy. He receives personally his reward, and he delivers personally his intelligence. We in France know something of the breed. There is still a chance, *mes amis*. These men must cross the sea, and there are ships to be searched and ports to be watched. Believe me, the need is desperate for both France and Britain."

Royer's grave good sense seemed to pull us together. He was the man of action among fumblers. But I saw no hope in any face, and I felt none. Where among the fifty millions of these islands and within a dozen hours were we to lay hands on the three cleverest rogues in Europe?

Then suddenly I had an inspiration.

"Where is Scudder's book?" I cried to Sir Walter. "Quick, man, I remember something in it."

He unlocked the door of a bureau and gave it to me.

I found the place. *Thirty-nine steps*, I read, and again,

2 **confederate:** Verbündete(r).

3 f. **not a rag of a clue:** nicht den geringsten Anhaltspunkt, nicht die geringste Spur.

16 **fumbler:** Stümper(in), Patzer(in).

19 **rogue:** Schurke, Gauner(in).

24 **bureau:** Schreibpult.

Thirty-nine steps – I counted them – High tide, 10.17 p.m.

The Admiralty man was looking at me as if he thought I had gone mad.

"Don't you see it's a clue," I shouted. "Scudder knew where these fellows laired – he knew where they were going to leave the country, though he kept the name to himself. To-morrow was the day, and it was some place where high tide was at 10.17."

"They may have gone to-night," someone said.

"Not they. They have their own snug secret way, and they won't be hurried. I know Germans, and they are mad about working to a plan. Where the devil can I get a book of Tide Tables?"

Whittaker brightened up. "It's a chance," he said. "Let's go over to the Admiralty."

We got into two of the waiting motor-cars – all but Sir Walter, who went off to Scotland Yard – to "mobilize MacGillivray", so he said.

We marched through empty corridors and big bare chambers where the charwomen were busy, till we reached a little room lined with books and maps. A resident clerk was unearthed, who presently fetched from the library the Admiralty Tide Tables. I sat at the desk and the others stood round, for somehow or other I had got charge of this expedition.

It was no good. There were hundreds of entries, and so

6 **to lair:** sich verstecken, sich aufhalten.
14 **tide table:** Gezeitentafel.
21 **charwoman:** Putzfrau.
23 **to unearth s.o.:** jdn. ausfindig machen, aufstöbern.

far as I could see 10.17 might cover fifty places. We had to find some way of narrowing the possibilities.

I took my head in my hands and thought. There must be some way of reading this riddle. What did Scudder mean by steps? I thought of dock steps, but if he had meant that I didn't think he would have mentioned the number. It must be some place where there were several staircases, and one marked out from the others by having thirty-nine steps.

Then I had a sudden thought, and hunted up all the steamer sailings. There was no boat which left for the Continent at 10.17 p.m.

Why was high tide important? If it was a harbour it must be some little place where the tide mattered, or else it was a heavy-draught boat. But there was no regular steamer sailing at that hour, and somehow I didn't think they would travel by a big boat from a regular harbour. So it must be some little harbour where the tide was important, or perhaps no harbour at all.

But if it was a little port I couldn't see what the steps signified. There were no sets of staircases on any harbour that I had ever seen. It must be some place which a particular staircase identified, and where the tide was full at 10.17. On the whole it seemed to me that the place must be a bit of open coast. But the staircases kept puzzling me.

Then I went back to wider considerations. Whereabouts would a man be likely to leave for Germany, a man in a hurry, who wanted a speedy and a secret passage? Not from any of the big harbours. And not from

15 **heavy-draught:** mit großem Tiefgang.

the Channel or the West Coast or Scotland, for, remember, he was starting from London. I measured the distance on the map, and tried to put myself in the enemy's shoes. I should try for Ostend or Antwerp or Rotterdam, and I should sail from somewhere on the East Coast between Cromer and Dover.

All this was very loose guessing, and I don't pretend it was ingenious or scientific. I wasn't any kind of Sherlock Holmes. But I have always fancied I had a kind of instinct about questions like this. I don't know if I can explain myself, but I used to use my brains as far as they went, and after they came to a blank wall I guessed, and I usually found my guesses pretty right.

So I set out all my conclusions on a bit of Admiralty paper. They ran like this:

FAIRLY CERTAIN

(1) Place where there are several sets of stairs; one that matters distinguished by having thirty-nine steps.
(2) Full tide at 10.17 P.M. Leaving shore only possible at full tide.
(3) Steps not dock steps, and so place probably not harbour.
(4) No regular night steamer at 10.17. Means of transport must be tramp (unlikely), yacht, or fishing-boat.

There my reasoning stopped. I made another list, which I headed "Guessed", but I was just as sure of the one as the other.

25 **tramp:** Trampschiff (Frachtschiff, das nicht auf festen Routen verkehrt).

GUESSED

(1) Place not harbour but open coast.
(2) Boat small – trawler, yacht, or launch.
(3) Place somewhere on East Coast between Cromer and Dover.

It struck me as odd that I should be sitting at that desk with a Cabinet Minister, a Field-Marshal, two high Government officials, and a French General watching me, while from the scribble of a dead man I was trying to drag a secret which meant life or death for us.

Sir Walter had joined us, and presently MacGillivray arrived. He had sent out instructions to watch the ports and railway stations for the three men whom I had described to Sir Walter. Not that he or anybody else thought that that would do much good.

"Here's the most I can make of it," I said. "We have got to find a place where there are several staircases down to the beach, one of which has thirty-nine steps. I think it's a piece of open coast with biggish cliffs, somewhere between the Wash and the Channel. Also it's a place where full tide is at 10.17 to-morrow night."

Then an idea struck me. "Is there no Inspector of Coastguards or some fellow like that who knows the East Coast?"

Whittaker said there was, and that he lived in Clapham.

3 **trawler:** Trawler (Fischereifangschiff mit einem Schleppnetz). **launch:** Barkasse, Motorboot.
9 **scribble:** Gekritzel.
20 **Wash:** Meeresbucht zwischen den Grafschaften Lincolnshire und Norfolk.
22 f. **Inspector of Coastguards:** Kommandant, Einsatzleiter der Küstenwache.
25 **Clapham:** Stadtteil im Südwesten von London.

He went off in a car to fetch him, and the rest of us sat about the little room and talked of anything that came into our heads. I lit a pipe and went over the whole thing again till my brain grew weary.

About one in the morning the coastguard man arrived. He was a fine old fellow, with the look of a naval officer, and was desperately respectful to the company. I left the War Minister to cross-examine him, for I felt he would think it cheek in me to talk.

"We want you to tell us the places you know on the East Coast where there are cliffs, and where several sets of steps run down to the beach."

He thought for a bit. "What kind of steps do you mean, sir? There are plenty of places with roads cut down through the cliffs, and most roads have a step or two in them. Or do you mean regular staircases – all steps, so to speak?"

Sir Arthur looked towards me. "We mean regular staircases," I said.

He reflected a minute or two. "I don't know that I can think of any. Wait a second. There's a place in Norfolk – Brattlesham – beside a golf-course, where there are a couple of staircases to let the gentlemen get a lost ball."

"That's not it," I said.

"Then there are plenty of Marine Parades, if that's what you mean. Every seaside resort has them."

9 **cheek** (infml.): Frechheit, Unverfrorenheit.
22 **Brattlesham:** fiktiver Name für einen Ort in der ostenglischen Grafschaft Norfolk.
26 **marine parade:** Seeuferpromenade.
27 **seaside resort:** Seebad.

I shook my head.
"It's got to be more retired than that," I said.
"Well, gentlemen, I can't think of anywhere else. Of course, there's the Ruff –"
"What's that?" I asked.
"The big chalk headland in Kent, close to Bradgate. It's got a lot of villas on the top, and some of the houses have staircases down to a private beach. It's a very high-toned sort of place, and the residents there like to keep by themselves."
I tore open the Tide Tables and found Bradgate. High tide there was at 10.27 p.m. on the 15th June.
"We're on the scent at last," I cried excitedly. "How can I find out what is the tide at the Ruff?"
"I can tell you that, sir," said the coastguard man. "I once was lent a house there in this very month, and I used to go out at night to the deep-sea fishing. The tide's ten minutes before Bradgate."
I closed the book and looked round at the company.
"If one of those staircases has thirty-nine steps we have solved the mystery, gentlemen," I said. "I want the loan of your car, Sir Walter, and a map of the roads. If Mr

2 **retired:** abgelegen, einsam.
4 **Ruff:** fiktiver Name für North Foreland, das östlichste Kap in der südostenglischen Grafschaft Kent. Das neugotische Herrenhaus darauf wurde vom dritten Lord Holland (1773–1840) gebaut, der den Ruf eines französischen Agenten in den Napoleonischen Kriegen (1793–1815) hatte.
6 **headland:** Landspitze.
Bradgate: fiktiver Name für das Seebad Broadstairs in Kent, wo die Buchans den Sommer 1914 verbrachten.
9 **high-toned:** vornehm.
13 **on the scent:** (fig.) auf der (richtigen) Fährte.

MacGillivray will spare me ten minutes, I think we can prepare something for to-morrow."

It was ridiculous in me to take charge of the business like this, but they didn't seem to mind, and after all I had been in the show from the start. Besides, I was used to rough jobs, and these eminent gentlemen were too clever not to see it. It was General Royer who gave me my commission. "I for one," he said, "am content to leave the matter in Mr Hannay's hands."

By half-past three I was tearing past the moonlit hedgerows of Kent, with MacGillivray's best man on the seat beside me.

Chapter X

Various Parties Converging on the Sea

A pink and blue June morning found me at Bradgate looking from the Griffin Hotel over a smooth sea to the lightship on the Cock sands which seemed the size of a bell-buoy. A couple of miles farther south and much nearer the shore a small destroyer was anchored. Scaife, MacGillivray's man, who had been in the navy,

6 **eminent:** bedeutend, angesehen.
10 **to tear past s.th.** (infml.): an etwas vorbeirasen, -sausen.
10 f. **hedgerow:** Hecke.
14 **to converge:** sich einander nähern, zusammenkommen.
17 **lightship:** Feuer-, Leuchtschiff.
18 **bell-buoy:** Glockenboje (Boje mit eingebauter Glocke).

knew the boat, and told me her name and her commander's, so I sent off a wire to Sir Walter.

After breakfast Scaife got from a house-agent a key for the gates of the staircases on the Ruff. I walked with him along the sands, and sat down in a nook of the cliffs while he investigated the half-dozen of them. I didn't want to be seen, but the place at this hour was quite deserted, and all the time I was on that beach I saw nothing but the sea-gulls.

It took him more than an hour to do the job, and when I saw him coming towards me, conning a bit of paper, I can tell you my heart was in my mouth. Everything depended, you see, on my guess proving right.

He read aloud the number of steps in the different stairs. "Thirty-four, thirty-five, thirty-nine, forty-two, forty-seven," and "twenty-one" where the cliffs grew lower. I almost got up and shouted.

We hurried back to the town and sent a wire to MacGillivray. I wanted half a dozen men, and I directed them to divide themselves among different specified hotels. Then Scaife set out to prospect the house at the head of the thirty-nine steps.

He came back with news that both puzzled and reassured me. The house was called Trafalgar Lodge, and belonged to an old gentlemen called Appleton – a re-

3 **house-agent:** Häusermakler(in).

9 **sea-gull:** Seemöwe.

23 f. **to reassure:** beruhigen.

24 **Trafalgar Lodge:** gemeint ist vermutl. ein Haus im edwardianischen Stil (aus der Regierungszeit König Edwards VII., 1901–10) namens St Cuby in Broadstairs, von dem aus ein Treppenschacht mit 107 Stufen zum Meer führt.

tired stockbroker, the house-agent said. Mr Appleton was there a good deal in the summer time, and was in residence now – had been for the better part of a week. Scaife could pick up very little information about him, except that he was a decent old fellow, who paid his bills regularly, and was always good for a fiver for a local charity. Then Scaife seems to have penetrated to the back door of the house, pretending he was an agent for sewing-machines. Only three servants were kept, a cook, a parlour-maid, and a housemaid, and they were just the sort that you would find in a respectable middle-class household. The cook was not the gossiping kind, and had pretty soon shut the door in his face, but Scaife said he was positive she knew nothing. Next door there was a new house building which would give good cover for observation, and the villa on the other side was to let, and its garden was rough and shrubby.

I borrowed Scaife's telescope, and before lunch went for a walk along the Ruff. I kept well behind the rows of villas, and found a good observation point on the edge of the golf-course. There I had a view of the line of turf along the cliff top, with seats placed at intervals, and the little square plots, railed in and planted with bushes, whence the staircases descended to the beach.

7 **charity:** Wohltätigkeit; Wohlfahrtseinrichtung.
9 **sewing-machine:** Nähmaschine.
10 **parlour-maid** (arch.): Hausangestellte, -mädchen.
12 **gossiping:** geschwätzig, schwatzhaft.
18 **shrubby:** mit Strauchwerk bewachsen.
23 **turf:** Rasen.
24 **plot:** Grundstück.

I saw Trafalgar Lodge very plainly, a red-brick villa with a veranda, a tennis lawn behind, and in front the ordinary seaside flower-garden full of marguerites and scraggy geraniums. There was a flagstaff from which an enormous Union Jack hung limply in the still air.

Presently I observed someone leave the house and saunter along the cliff. When I got my glasses on him I saw it was an old man, wearing white flannel trousers, a blue serge jacket, and a straw hat. He carried field-glasses and a newspaper, and sat down on one of the iron seats and began to read. Sometimes he would lay down the paper and turn his glasses on the sea. He looked for a long time at the destroyer. I watched him for half an hour, till he got up and went back to the house for his luncheon, when I returned to the hotel for mine.

I wasn't feeling very confident. This decent common-place dwelling was not what I had expected. The man might be the bald archaeologist of that horrible moor-land farm, or he might not. He was exactly the kind of satisfied old bird you will find in every suburb and every holiday place. If you wanted a type of the perfectly harmless person you would probably pitch on that.

But after lunch, as I sat in the hotel porch, I perked up,

1 **red-brick:** Backstein.
4 **scraggy:** dürr, knorrig.
flagstaff: Fahnenstange, Flaggenmast.
5 **Union Jack:** britische Nationalflagge.
limply (adv.): schlaff.
21 **old bird** (infml.): alter Knabe.
23 **to pitch on s.o.:** auf jdn. verfallen, sich an jdn. ranmachen.
24 **to perk up:** den Kopf recken, die Ohren spitzen, munter werden.

for I saw the thing I had hoped for and had dreaded to miss. A yacht came up from the south and dropped anchor pretty well opposite the Ruff. She seemed about a hundred and fifty tons, and I saw she belonged to the Squadron from the white ensign. So Scaife and I went down to the harbour and hired a boatman for an afternoon's fishing.

I spent a warm and peaceful afternoon. We caught between us about twenty pounds of cod and lythe, and out in that dancing blue sea I took a cheerier view of things. Above the white cliffs of the Ruff I saw the green and red of the villas, and especially the great flagstaff of Trafalgar Lodge. About four o'clock, when we had fished enough, I made the boatman row us round the yacht, which lay like a delicate white bird, ready at a moment to flee. Scaife said she must be a fast boat from her build, and that she was pretty heavily engined.

Her name was the *Ariadne*, as I discovered from the cap of one of the men who was polishing brasswork. I spoke to him, and got an answer in the soft dialect of Essex. Another hand that came along passed me the time of day in an unmistakable English tongue. Our boatman had an argument with one of them about the

5 **Squadron:** gemeint ist vermutl. das in Cowes auf der Isle of Wight ansässige Royal Yacht Squadron oder der Royal Yacht Club mit sehr reichen Mitgliedern.
white ensign: Flagge der britischen Kriegsmarine.
9 **cod:** Kabeljau, Dorsch.
lythe (Scot.): Schellfisch.
20 **brasswork:** Messingarmaturen.
22 **Essex:** Grafschaft nordöstlich von London.

weather, and for a few minutes we lay on our oars close to the starboard bow.

Then the men suddenly disregarded us and bent their heads to their work as an officer came along the deck. He was a pleasant, clean-looking young fellow, and he put a question to us about our fishing in very good English. But there could be no doubt about him. His close-cropped head and the cut of his collar and tie never came out of England.

That did something to reassure me, but as we rowed back to Bradgate my obstinate doubts would not be dismissed. The thing that worried me was the reflection that my enemies knew that I had got my knowledge from Scudder, and it was Scudder who had given me the clue to this place. If they knew that Scudder had this clue, would they not be certain to change their plans? Too much depended on their success for them to take any risks. The whole question was how much they understood about Scudder's knowledge. I had talked confidently last night about Germans always sticking to a scheme, but if they had any suspicions that I was on their track they would be fools not to cover it. I wondered if the man last night had seen that I recognized him. Somehow I did not think he had, and to that I clung. But the whole business had never seemed so difficult as that afternoon when by all

1 **to lie on one's oars:** die Riemen hoch nehmen; (fig.) sich ausruhen.

2 **starboard:** Steuerbord; steuerbordseitig.
bow: (Schiffs-)Bug.

8 **close-cropped:** mit kurzgeschnittenem Haar.

11 **obstinate:** hartnäckig.

calculations I should have been rejoicing in assured success.

In the hotel I met the commander of the destroyer, to whom Scaife introduced me, and with whom I had a few words. Then I thought I would put in an hour or two watching Trafalgar Lodge.

I found a place farther up the hill, in the garden of an empty house. From there I had a full view of the court, on which two figures were having a game of tennis. One was the old man, whom I had already seen; the other was a younger fellow, wearing some club colours in the scarf round his middle. They played with tremendous zest, like two city gents who wanted hard exercise to open their pores. You couldn't conceive a more innocent spectacle. They shouted and laughed and stopped for drinks, when a maid brought out two tankards on a salver. I rubbed my eyes and asked myself if I was not the most immortal fool on earth. Mystery and darkness had hung about the men who hunted me over the Scotch moor in aeroplane and motor-car, and notably about that infernal antiquarian. It was easy enough to connect those folk with the knife that pinned Scudder to the floor, and with fell designs on the world's peace.

1 **to rejoice in s.th.:** sich einer Sache erfreuen; (fig.) sich mit etwas schmücken.
11 **club colours:** Vereinsfarben.
13 **zest:** Lust, Freude, Begeisterung, Schwung.
14 **pore:** (Haut-)Pore.
16 **tankard:** (Bier-)Krug, Humpen.
17 **salver:** Tablett.
21 **antiquarian:** Altertumsforscher(in).
23 **fell:** grausam, wild, mörderisch, tödlich.

But here were two guileless citizens taking their innocuous exercise, and soon about to go indoors to a humdrum dinner, where they would talk of market prices and the last cricket scores and the gossip of their native Surbiton. I had been making a net to catch vultures and falcons, and lo and behold! two plump thrushes had blundered into it.

Presently a third figure arrived, a young man on a bicycle, with a bag of golf-clubs slung on his back. He strolled round to the tennis lawn and was welcomed riotously by the players. Evidently they were chaffing him, and their chaff sounded horribly English. Then the plump man, mopping his brow with a silk handkerchief, announced that he must have a tub. I heard his very words – "I've got into a proper lather," he said. "This will bring down my weight and my handicap, Bob. I'll take you on to-morrow and give you a stroke

1 **guileless:** arglos, harmlos, ohne Falsch.
1 f. **innocuous:** unschädlich, harmlos.
2 f. **humdrum:** langweilig.
5 **Surbiton:** spez.: Londoner Vorort; allg.: typisch englischer Vorort (Wortspiel mit *suburb*).
vulture: Geier.
6 **falcon:** Falke.
thrush: Drossel.
7 **to blunder:** tappen.
10 **to stroll:** spazieren, schlendern.
11 **riotously** (adv.): ausgelassen, wild.
to chaff: necken, aufziehen.
14 **tub** (infml.): (Wannen-)Bad.
15 **to get into a lather:** schweißgebadet sein.
17 **to take s.o. on:** jdn. als Gegner(in) annehmen, es mit jdm. aufnehmen, den Kampf mit jdm. aufnehmen.
17 f. **to give s.o. a stroke a hole:** jdm. (beim Golf) einen Vorteil geben.

a hole." You couldn't find anything much more English than that.

They all went into the house, and left me feeling a precious idiot. I had been barking up the wrong tree this time. These men might be acting; but if they were, where was their audience? They didn't know I was sitting thirty yards off in a rhododendron. It was simply impossible to believe that these three hearty fellows were anything but what they seemed – three ordinary, game-playing, suburban Englishmen, wearisome, if you like, but sordidly innocent.

And yet there were three of them; and one was old, and one was plump, and one was lean and dark; and their house chimed in with Scudder's notes; and half a mile off was lying a steam yacht with at least one German officer. I thought of Karolides lying dead and all Europe trembling on the edge of earthquake, and the men I had left behind me in London who were waiting anxiously for the events of the next hours. There was no doubt that hell was afoot somewhere. The Black Stone had won, and if it survived this June night would bank its winnings.

4 **to bark up the wrong tree** (fig.): auf dem Holzweg, an der falschen Adresse sein.
8 **hearty:** herzlich, jovial, munter, begeistert.
10 **suburban:** Vorort-, vorstädtisch; (fig.) spießig.
wearisome: ermüdend, langweilig.
11 **sordidly** (adv.): hier: etwa: stink-.
14 **to chime in with s.th.:** mit etwas übereinstimmen.
17 **earthquake:** Erdbeben.
22 **to bank one's winnings:** seinen (Spiel-)Gewinn einlösen; (fig.) sich absetzen, verschwinden.

There seemed only one thing to do – go forward as if I had no doubts, and if I was going to make a fool of myself to do it handsomely. Never in my life have I faced a job with greater disinclination. I would rather in my then mind have walked into a den of anarchists, each with his Browning handy, or faced a charging lion with a popgun, than enter that happy home of three cheerful Englishmen and tell them that their game was up. How they would laugh at me!

But suddenly I remembered a thing I once heard in Rhodesia from old Peter Pienaar. I have quoted Peter already in this narrative. He was the best scout I ever knew, and before he had turned respectable he had been pretty often on the windy side of the law, when he had been wanted badly by the authorities. Peter once discussed with me the question of disguises, and he had a theory which struck me at the time. He said, barring absolute certainties like fingerprints, mere physical traits were very little use for identification if the fugitive really knew his business. He laughed at things like dyed hair and false beards and such childish follies. The only thing that mattered was what Peter called "ammosphere".

If a man could get into perfectly different surroundings from those in which he had been first observed, and – this is the important part – really play up to these sur-

4 **disinclination:** Abneigung, Unlust.
5 **den:** Höhle; (pej.) Loch.
6 **Browning:** Name einer Pistole.
7 **popgun:** Kindergewehr, Knallbüchse, schlechtes Gewehr.
17 **barring:** abgesehen von, ausgenommen.
19 **trait:** Eigenschaft, Merkmal.

roundings and behave as if he had never been out of them, he would puzzle the cleverest detectives on earth. And he used to tell a story of how he once borrowed a black coat and went to church and shared the same hymn-book with the man that was looking for him. If that man had seen him in decent company before he would have recognized him; but he had only seen him snuffing the lights in a public-house with a revolver.

The recollection of Peter's talk gave me the first real comfort I had had that day. Peter had been a wise old bird, and these fellows I was after were about the pick of the aviary. What if they were playing Peter's game? A fool tries to look different: a clever man looks the same and *is* different.

Again, there was that other maxim of Peter's which had helped me when I had been a roadman. "If you are playing a part, you will never keep it up unless you convince yourself that you are *it*." That would explain the game of tennis. Those chaps didn't need to act, they just turned a handle and passed into another life, which came as naturally to them as the first. It sounds a platitude, but Peter used to say that it was the big secret of all the famous criminals.

It was now getting on for eight o'clock, and I went back and saw Scaife to give him his instructions. I arranged with him how to place his men, and then I went for a

8 **to snuff:** (aus)löschen.
12 **pick:** Elite, Beste(r, -s).
13 **aviary:** Vogelhaus, Voliere.
16 **maxim:** Maxime, Leitsatz.
22 f. **platitude:** Platitüde, Plattheit, Gemeinplatz.

walk, for I didn't feel up to any dinner. I went round the deserted golf-course, and then to a point on the cliffs farther north beyond the line of the villas.

On the little trim newly-made roads I met people in flannels coming back from tennis and the beach, and a coastguard from the wireless station, and donkeys and pierrots padding homewards. Out at sea in the blue dusk I saw lights appear on the *Ariadne* and on the destroyer away to the south, and beyond the Cock sands the bigger lights of steamers making for the Thames. The whole scene was so peaceful and ordinary that I got more dashed in spirits every second. It took all my resolution to stroll towards Trafalgar Lodge about half-past nine.

On the way I got a piece of solid comfort from the sight of a greyhound that was swinging along at a nurse-maid's heels. He reminded me of a dog I used to have in Rhodesia, and of the time when I took him hunting with me in the Pali hills. We were after rhebok, the dun kind, and I recollected how we had followed one beast, and both he and I had clean lost it. A greyhound works by sight, and my eyes are good enough, but that buck

4 **trim:** ordentlich, gepflegt, sauber, schmuck.
7 **pierrot** (Fr.): Pierrot (komische Figur in der französischen Pantomime), Hanswurst, Clown; hier: Artist eines Strandvarietés.
to pad (slang): trotten, latschen.
12 **dashed:** verwirrt, deprimiert.
16 **greyhound:** englischer Windhund.
19 **Pali hills** (pl.): Hügelkette in Rhodesien (Simbabwe).
rhebok (S. Afr.): Antilopenart.
20 **to recollect:** sich erinnern.
22 **buck:** (Hirsch-, Reh-)Bock.

simply leaked out of the landscape. Afterwards I found out how it managed it. Against the grey rock of the kopjes it showed no more than a crow against a thundercloud. It didn't need to run away; all it had to do was to stand still and melt into the background. Suddenly as these memories chased across my brain I thought of my present case and applied the moral. The Black Stone didn't need to bolt. They were quietly absorbed into the landscape. I was on the right track, and I jammed that down in my mind and vowed never to forget it. The last word was with Peter Pienaar.

Scaife's men would be posted now, but there was no sign of a soul. The house stood as open as a marketplace for anybody to observe. A three-foot railing separated it from the cliff road; the windows on the groundfloor were all open, and shaded lights and the low sound of voices revealed where the occupants were finishing dinner. Everything was as public and aboveboard as a charity bazaar. Feeling the greatest fool on earth, I opened the gate and rang the bell.

A man of my sort, who has travelled about the world in rough places, gets on perfectly well with two classes, what you may call the upper and the lower. He understands them and they understand him. I was at home with herds and tramps and roadmen, and I was suffi-

1 **to leak:** entweichen, spurlos verschwinden.
3 **kopje** (S. Afr.): kleiner (einzeln herausragender) Hügel, Berg.
8 **to bolt:** ausreißen, davonlaufen, durchbrennen.
10 **to vow:** schwören.
18 f. **above-board:** offen, ehrlich, einwandfrei.

ciently at my ease with people like Sir Walter and the men I had met the night before. I can't explain why, but it is a fact. But what fellows like me don't understand is the great comfortable, satisfied middle-class world, the folk that live in villas and suburbs. He doesn't know how they look at things, he doesn't understand their conventions, and he is as shy of them as of a black mamba. When a trim parlour-maid opened the door, I could hardly find my voice.

I asked for Mr Appleton, and was ushered in. My plan had been to walk straight into the dining-room, and by a sudden appearance wake in the men that start of recognition which would confirm my theory. But when I found myself in that neat hall the place mastered me. There were the golf-clubs and tennis-rackets, the straw hats and caps, the rows of gloves, the sheaf of walking-sticks, which you will find in ten thousand British homes. A stack of neatly folded coats and waterproofs covered the top of an old oak chest; there was a grandfather clock ticking; and some polished brass warming-pans on the walls, and a barometer, and a print of Chiltern winning the St Leger. The place was as orthodox as an Anglican church. When the maid asked me for

7 f. **black mamba:** Schwarze Mamba (Giftnatter).

16 **sheaf:** Bündel, Garbe.

19 f. **grandfather clock:** Standuhr.

21 f. **Chiltern:** Name des ersten Vollblutpferdes.

22 **St Leger:** seit 1776 jährlich in Doncaster in der Grafschaft Südyorkshire stattfindendes Pferderennen.

23 **Anglican:** anglikanisch, auf die Church of England und die anderen mit ihr in Verbindung stehenden britischen und irischen Kirchen bezogen.

my name I gave it automatically, and was shown into the smoking-room, on the right side of the hall.

That room was even worse. I hadn't time to examine it, but I could see some framed group photographs above the mantelpiece, and I could have sworn they were English public school or college. I had only one glance, for I managed to pull myself together and go after the maid. But I was too late. She had already entered the dining-room and given my name to her master, and I had missed the chance of seeing how the three took it.

When I walked into the room the old man at the head of the table had risen and turned round to meet me. He was in evening dress – a short coat and black tie, as was the other, whom I called in my own mind the plump one. The third, the dark fellow, wore a blue serge suit and a soft white collar, and the colours of some club or school.

The old man's manner was perfect. "Mr Hannay?" he said hesitatingly. "Did you wish to see me? One moment, you fellows, and I'll rejoin you. We had better go to the smoking-room."

Though I hadn't an ounce of confidence in me, I forced myself to play the game. I pulled up a chair and sat down on it.

"I think we have met before," I said, "and I guess you know my business."

5 **mantelpiece:** Einfassung eines (offenen) Kamins, Kaminsims.

15 f. **the plump one:** Die Figur des Untersetzten taucht als Moxon Ivery, Graf von Schwabing, in Buchans Roman *Mr Standfast* wieder auf.

21 **to rejoin s.o.:** wieder zu jdm. stoßen.

The light in the room was dim, but so far as I could see their faces, they played the part of mystification very well.

"Maybe, maybe," said the old man. "I haven't a very good memory, but I'm afraid you must tell me your errand, sir, for I really don't know it."

"Well, then," I said, and all the time I seemed to myself to be talking pure foolishness – "I have come to tell you that the game's up. I have here a warrant for the arrest of you three gentlemen."

"Arrest," said the old man, and he looked really shocked. "Arrest! Good God, what for?"

"For the murder of Franklin Scudder in London on the 23rd day of last month."

"I never heard the name before," said the old man in a dazed voice.

One of the others spoke up. "That was the Portland Place murder. I read about it. Good heavens, you must be mad, sir! Where do you come from?"

"Scotland Yard," I said.

After that for a minute there was utter silence. The old man was staring at his plate and fumbling with a nut, the very model of innocent bewilderment.

Then the plump one spoke up. He stammered a little, like a man picking his words.

"Don't get flustered, uncle," he said. "It is all a ridicu-

2 **mystification:** Verwirrung.
5 f. **errand:** Auftrag.
9 **warrant:** Vollmacht, Haftbefehl.
16 **dazed:** benommen.
23 **bewilderment:** Verwirrung, Bestürzung.
26 **to get flustered:** nervös werden, sich aufregen.

lous mistake; but these things happen sometimes, and we can easily set it right. It won't be hard to prove our innocence. I can show that I was out of the country on the 23rd of May, and Bob was in a nursing home. You were in London, but you can explain what you were doing."

"Right, Percy! Of course that's easy enough. The 23rd! That was the day after Agatha's wedding. Let me see. What was I doing? I came up in the morning from Woking, and lunched at the club with Charlie Symons. Then – oh yes, I dined with the Fishmongers. I remember, for the punch didn't agree with me, and I was seedy next morning. Hang it all, there's the cigar-box I brought back from the dinner." He pointed to an object on the table, and laughed nervously.

"I think, sir," said the young man, addressing me respectfully, "you will see you are mistaken. We want to assist the law like all Englishmen, and we don't want Scotland Yard to be making fools of themselves. That's so, uncle?"

"Certainly, Bob." The old fellow seemed to be recovering his voice. "Certainly, we'll do anything in our power to assist the authorities. But – but this is a bit too much. I can't get over it."

"How Nellie will chuckle," said the plump man. "She

4 **nursing home:** Privatklinik.
9 f. **Woking:** Stadt südwestlich von London in der Grafschaft Surrey.
11 **Fishmongers** (pl.): Handelszunft in der City of London mit einem Clubrestaurant.
12 **punch:** Punsch.
to be seedy (infml.): sich mies, angeschlagen fühlen.
25 **to chuckle:** leise lachen, in sich hineinlachen; sich (insgeheim) freuen.

always said that you would die of boredom because nothing ever happened to you. And now you've got it thick and strong," and he began to laugh very pleasantly.

"By Jove, yes. Just think of it! What a story to tell at the club. Really, Mr Hannay, I suppose I should be angry, to show my innocence, but it's too funny! I almost forgive you the fright you gave me! You looked so glum, I thought I might have been walking in my sleep and killing people."

It couldn't be acting, it was too confoundedly genuine. My heart went into my boots, and my first impulse was to apologize and clear out. But I told myself I must see it through, even though I was to be the laughing-stock of Britain. The light from the dinner-table candlesticks was not very good, and to cover my confusion I got up, walked to the door and switched on the electric light. The sudden glare made them blink, and I stood scanning the three faces.

Well, I made nothing of it. One was old and bald, one was stout, one was dark and thin. There was nothing in their appearance to prevent them being the three who had hunted me in Scotland, but there was nothing to identify them. I simply can't explain why I who, as a roadman, had looked into two pairs of eyes, and as

3 **thick and strong** (fig.): viel zuviel.
5 **by Jove:** Donnerwetter!, beim Zeus (Jupiter)!
11 **confoundedly** (adv.): verdammt.
13 f. **to see it through:** die Sache (bis zum Ende) durchhalten, -fechten.
14 **laughing-stock:** Gegenstand des Gelächters, Zielscheibe des Spottes.
18 **glare:** grelles Licht.

Ned Ainslie into another pair, why I, who have a good memory and reasonable powers of observation, could find no satisfaction. They seemed exactly what they professed to be, and I could not have sworn to one of them.

There in that pleasant dining-room, with etchings on the walls, and a picture of an old lady in a bib above the mantelpiece, I could see nothing to connect them with the moorland desperadoes. There was a silver cigarette-box beside me, and I saw that it had been won by Percival Appleton, Esq., of the St Bede's Club, in a golf tournament. I had to keep firm hold of Peter Pienaar to prevent myself bolting out of that house.

"Well," said the old man politely, "are you reassured by your scrutiny, sir?"

I couldn't find a word.

"I hope you'll find it consistent with your duty to drop this ridiculous business. I make no complaint, but you'll see how annoying it must be to respectable people."

I shook my head.

"O Lord," said the young man. "This is a bit too thick!"

"Do you propose to march us off to the police station?" asked the plump one. "That might be the best way out of it, but I suppose you won't be content with the local branch. I have the right to ask to see your warrant, but

4 **to profess to be s.th.:** behaupten, etwas zu sein.
6 **etching:** Radierung, Kupferstich.
7 **bib:** Schürzenlatz.
11 **Esq.:** Abk. für *Esquire:* Herr.
15 **scrutiny:** (genaue) Untersuchung.
17 **consistent:** vereinbar.

I don't wish to cast any aspersions upon you. You are only doing your duty. But you'll admit it's horribly awkward. What do you propose to do?"

There was nothing to do except to call in my men and have them arrested, or to confess my blunder and clear out. I felt mesmerized by the whole place, by the air of obvious innocence – not innocence merely, but frank honest bewilderment and concern in the three faces.

"Oh, Peter Pienaar," I groaned inwardly, and for a moment I was very near damning myself for a fool and asking their pardon.

"Meantime I vote we have a game of bridge," said the plump one. "It will give Mr Hannay time to think over things, and you know we have been wanting a fourth player. Do you play, sir?"

I accepted as if it had been an ordinary invitation at the club. The whole business had mesmerized me. We went into the smoking-room where a card-table was set out, and I was offered things to smoke and drink. I took my place at the table in a kind of dream. The window was open and the moon was flooding the cliffs and sea with a great tide of yellow light. There was moonshine, too, in my head. The three had recovered their composure, and were talking easily – just the kind of slangy talk you hear in any golf club-house. I must have cut a rum

1 **to cast aspersions upon s.o.:** jdn. verleumden, mit Schmutz bewerfen.
5 **blunder:** grober Fehler.
6 **air:** Anschein.
23 **composure:** (Gemüts-)Ruhe, Gelassenheit, Fassung.
24 **slangy:** salopp.
25 **rum** (slang): komisch.

figure, sitting there knitting my brows with my eyes wandering.

My partner was the young dark one. I play a fair hand at bridge, but I must have been rank bad that night. They saw that they had got me puzzled, and that put them more than ever at their ease. I kept looking at their faces, but they conveyed nothing to me. It was not that they looked different; they *were* different. I clung desperately to the words of Peter Pienaar.

Then something awoke me.

The old man laid down his hand to light a cigar. He didn't pick it up at once, but sat back for a moment in his chair, with his fingers tapping on his knees.

It was the movement I remembered when I had stood before him in the moorland farm, with the pistols of his servants behind me.

A little thing, lasting only a second, and the odds were a thousand to one that I might have had my eyes on my cards at the time and missed it. But I didn't, and, in a flash, the air seemed to clear. Some shadow lifted from my brain, and I was looking at the three men with full and absolute recognition.

The clock on the mantelpiece struck ten o'clock.

The three faces seemed to change before my eyes and reveal their secrets. The young one was the murderer. Now I saw cruelty and ruthlessness, where before I had

1 **to knit one's brows:** die Stirn runzeln.
4 **rank:** kraß.
26 **ruthlessness:** Unbarmherzigkeit, Rücksichtslosigkeit, Skrupellosigkeit.

only seen goodhumour. His knife, I made certain, had skewered Scudder to the floor. His kind had put the bullet in Karolides.

The plump man's features seemed to dislimn, and form again, as I looked at them. He hadn't a face, only a hundred masks that he could assume when he pleased. That chap must have been a superb actor. Perhaps he had been Lord Alloa of the night before; perhaps not; it didn't matter. I wondered if he was the fellow who had first tracked Scudder, and left his card on him. Scudder had said he lisped, and I could imagine how the adoption of a lisp might add terror.

But the old man was the pick of the lot. He was sheer brain, icy, cool, calculating, as ruthless as a steam hammer. Now that my eyes were opened I wondered where I had seen the benevolence. His jaw was like chilled steel, and his eyes had the inhuman luminosity of a bird's. I went on playing, and every second a greater hate welled up in my heart. It almost choked me, and I couldn't answer when my partner spoke. Only a little longer could I endure their company.

"Whew! Bob! Look at the time," said the old man. "You'd better think about catching your train. Bob's got to go to town to-night," he added, turning to me. The voice rang now as false as hell.

2 **his kind:** Leute wie er.
4 **to dislimn** (poet.): (fig.) (sich) auslöschen, verlöschen.
10 **to leave one's card on s.o.** (iron.): seine Visitenkarte bei jdm. hinterlassen.
16 **benevolence:** Wohlwollen.
17 **luminosity:** Leuchten, Glanz.
22 **whew!:** Ausruf des Erstaunens; etwa: hui!, Mann!

I looked at the clock, and it was nearly half-past ten.

"I am afraid he must put off his journey," I said.

"Oh, damn," said the young man, "I thought you had dropped that rot. I've simply got to go. You can have my address, and I'll give any security you like."

"No," I said, "you must stay."

At that I think they must have realized that the game was desperate. Their only chance had been to convince me that I was playing the fool, and that had failed. But the old man spoke again.

"I'll go bail for my nephew. That ought to content you, Mr Hannay." Was it fancy, or did I detect some halt in the smoothness of that voice?

There must have been, for as I glanced at him, his eyelids fell in that hawk-like hood which fear had stamped on my memory.

I blew my whistle.

In an instant the lights were out. A pair of strong arms gripped me round the waist, covering the pockets in which a man might be expected to carry a pistol.

"*Schnell, Franz,*" cried a voice. "*Das Boot, das Boot!*"

As it spoke I saw two of my fellows emerge on the moonlit lawn.

The young dark man leapt for the window, was through it, and over the low fence before a hand could touch him. I grappled the old chap, and the room seemed to fill with figures. I saw the plump one collared, but my

11 **to go bail for s.o.:** für jdn. Sicherheit leisten, Kaution stellen.
12 **halt:** Pause, Unterbrechung; Holpern; Zögern.
15 **hood:** Haube, Kappe; gemeint ist viell. *mood.*
26 **to grapple:** packen, fassen.
27 **to collar s.o.:** jdn. beim Kragen packen, fassen, festnehmen.

eyes were all for the out-of-doors, where Franz sped on over the road towards the railed entrance to the beach stairs. One man followed him, but he had no chance. The gate of the stairs locked behind the fugitive, and I stood staring, with my hands on the old boy's throat, for such a time as a man might take to descend those steps to the sea.

Suddenly my prisoner broke from me and flung himself on the wall. There was a click as if a lever had been pulled. Then came a low rumbling far, far below the ground, and through the window I saw a cloud of chalky dust pouring out of the shaft of the stairway. Someone switched on the light.

The old man was looking at me with blazing eyes.

"He is safe," he cried. "You cannot follow in time. . . . He is gone. . . . He has triumphed. . . . *Der schwarze Stein ist in der Siegeskrone.*"

There was more in those eyes than any common triumph. They had been hooded like a bird of prey, and now they flamed with a hawk's pride. A white fanatic heat burned in them, and I realized for the first time the terrible thing I had been up against. This man was more than a spy; in his foul way he had been a patriot.

9 **lever:** Hebel.

10 **rumbling:** Gepolter, Rumpeln; (Donner-)Grollen. Siehe hierzu John Bunyan über den Höllenschlund in *The Pilgrim's Progress* (1768): »[. . .] the bottomless pit opened, just whereabout I stood; out of the mouth of which there came in an abundant manner smoke, and coals of fire, and hideous noises.«

12 **shaft:** Schacht.

As the handcuffs clinked on his wrists I said my last word to him.
"I hope Franz will bear his triumph well. I ought to tell you that the *Ariadne* for the last hour has been in our hands."

Three weeks later, as all the world knows, we went to war. I joined the New Army the first week, and owing to my Matabele experience got a captain's commission straight off. But I had done my best service, I think, before I put on khaki.

1 **handcuffs:** Handschellen.
to clink: klirren; klimpern.
7 **New Army:** durch den Aufruf des neuen Kriegsministers Earl Kitchener 1914 ins Leben gerufene Freiwilligenarmee.
10 **khaki:** Khaki (gelbbrauner [Uniform-]Stoff).

Editorische Notiz

Der englische Text folgt der Ausgabe: John Buchan, *The Thirty-Nine Steps*, edited with an introduction by Christopher Harvie, Oxford: Oxford University Press, 1993 (The World's Classics). Das Glossar erklärt in der Regel alle Wörter, die nicht in *Reclams Englischem Wörterbuch* von Dieter Hamblock (Stuttgart: Reclam, 1996) verzeichnet sind.

Im Glossar verwendete Abkürzungen

adv.	adverb
AE	American English
arch.	archaic (veraltet)
BE	British English
dial.	dialectal (mundartlich)
fig.	figuratively (übertragen)
Fr.	French
hum.	humorously (scherzhaft)
infml.	informal (umgangssprachlich)
Ir.	Irish
iron.	ironical
Lat.	Latin
milit.	military (Militär)
o.s.	oneself
pej.	pejorative (abschätzig)
pl.	plural
poet.	poetical (dichterisch, gehoben)
S. Afr.	South African
Scot./schott.	Scottish/schottisch
s.o.	someone
s.th.	something

Bio-bibliographische Angaben

JOHN BUCHAN, LORD TWEEDSMUIR

Geb. am 26. August 1875 in Perth (Schottland) als Sohn eines Pfarrers. Buchan verbrachte seine Jugend teilweise in den Gemeinden seines Vaters in den Industrieregionen Fife und Glasgow und teilweise auf der Farm der Familie seiner Mutter im Tal des Upper Tweed in der Borders-Region, dem Gebiet, in dem ein Großteil der Handlung von *The Thirty-Nine Steps* angesiedelt ist. Er besuchte zunächst die Universität Glasgow, anschließend die Universität Oxford und war bereits vor seinem Abschlußexamen ein produktiver Journalist und Literaturwissenschaftler. Da er eine politische Karriere anstrebte, arbeitete er in der Zeit nach dem Burenkrieg als Assistent von Sir Alfred Milner, dem Generalgouverneur von Südafrika. 1903 kehrte Buchan nach Großbritannien zurück, wo er 1907 Susan Grosvenor heiratete und Direktor des Nelson-Verlags in Edinburgh wurde. Er war damals bereits als Biograph, Historiker und Romanautor tätig, und sowohl seine politischen Interessen als auch sein Wissen über Deutschland machten ihn zu einer wichtigen Figur des geheimen Nachrichtendiensts im Ersten Weltkrieg, dessen Ende er als Staatssekretär im Informationsministerium erlebte. 1927 trat er als konservativer Abgeordneter der schottischen Universitäten in das Parlament ein, obwohl seine politische Grundhaltung eher zentrumsnah war. 1936 erwarb Buchan den Titel Lord Tweedsmuir und wurde zum Generalgouverneur von Kanada ernannt. Er starb am 11. Februar 1940 in Montreal. Zu diesem Zeitpunkt hatte Buchan über 100 Bücher veröffentlicht, von denen viele nach wie vor gedruckt werden. Diese gliedern sich im wesentlichen in Biographien, wie beispielsweise Studien über Augustus, Cromwell, Montrose und Sir Walter Scott, ferner historische Romane, wie z. B. *Witch Wood*, der von Satanskult und religiösem Fanatismus im Schottland des

17. Jahrhunderts handelt und als anerkanntes Meisterwerk gilt, und schließlich Polit-Thriller. Letztere weisen ein nahezu konstantes Arsenal von Figuren auf, das von Helden wie Richard Hannay, Dickson MacCunn, einem Lebensmittelhändler aus Glasgow, und dem halb autobiographischen Edward Leithen dominiert wird. Die Serie der Polit-Thriller begann 1913 mit *The Power House* und wurde bis 1936 fast jährlich fortgesetzt. Ihre gewandte, täuschend einfache Prosa, ihr Sinn für Atmosphäre und ihr Blick für die landschaftliche Szenerie haben Generationen von Lesern erfreut, für die die dargestellten gesellschaftlichen Kreise der Clubs und Jagdhüttenbesitzer oder auch der Mitglieder der Free Kirks und schottischen Facharbeiter so unerreichbar sind wie P. G. Wodehouses Drones Club.

Thriller: *Prester John (The Great Diamond Pipe)* (1910); *The Thirty-Nine Steps* (1915); *The Power House* (1916); *Greenmantle* (1916); *Mr Standfast* (1919); *The Three Hostages* (1924); *John Macnab* (1925); *The Dancing Floor* (1926); *The Courts of the Morning* (1929); *Castle Gay* (1930); *A Prince of the Captivity* (1933); *The House of the Four Winds* (1935); *The Island of Sheep (The Man from the Norlands)* (1936).
Historische Romane: *Sir Quixote of the Moors* (1895); *John Burnet of Barns* (1898); *A Lost Lady of Old Years* (1899); *Salute to Adventurers* (1915); *Midwinter* (1923); *Witch Wood* (1927); *The Blanket of the Dark* (1931); *The Free Fishers* (1934).
Romane: *The Half-Hearted* (1900); *Sick Heart River* (1941).
Geschichtliche Abhandlungen: *Nelson's History of the War* (1915–19); *The King's Grace* (1935).
Biographien: *The Marquis of Montrose* (1913); *Andrew Jameson, Lord Ardwall* (1913); *Montrose* (1928); *Sir Walter Scott* (1932); *Julius Caesar* (1932); *Oliver Cromwell* (1934); *Augustus* (1937); *Memory Hold-the-Door* (1940).
Essays: *Homilies and Recreations* (1926; Essays und Reden); *The Novel and the Fairy Tale* (1931; Literaturkritik).

Kurzprosasammlungen: *Grey Weather* (1899; Kurzgeschichten und Gedichte); *The Watcher by the Threshold* (1902); *The Moon Endureth* (1912; Kurzgeschichten und Gedichte); *The Path of the King* (1921); *The Runagates Club* (1928); *The Gap in the Curtain* (1932).
Lyriksammlungen: *Poems, Scots and English* (1917); *The Northern Muse* (1924).

Literaturhinweise

Beesly, Patrick, *Room 40: British Naval Intelligence, 1914–1918*, Oxford: Oxford University Press, 1982.

Buchan, J. W. H. de l'A., »John Buchan and the Great War«, in: *The John Buchan Journal* 7 (Winter 1987) S. 2–9.

Clarke, I. F., *Voices Prophesying War*, London: Panther, 1969 ([1]1966).

Daniell, David, *The Interpreter's House: A Critical Assessment of John Buchan*, London: Nelson, 1975.

Harvie, Christopher, *The Centre of Things: Political Fiction in Britain from Disraeli to the Present*, London: Unwin Hyman, 1991.

– »Second Thoughts of a Scotsman on the Make: Politics, Nationalism and Myth in John Buchan«, in: *The Scottish Historical Review* 70 (1991), Heft 188, S. 31–54.

Klotz, Volker, *Abenteuer-Romane*, München: Hanser, 1979.

Palmer, Jerry, *Thrillers*, London: Edward Arnold, 1978.

Smith, Janet Adam, *John Buchan: A Biography*, Oxford: Oxford University Press, 1985 ([1]1965).

Stafford, David T., »John Buchan's Tales of Espionage: A Popular Archive of British History«, in: *Canadian Journal of History* 18 (1983), Heft 2, S. 1–23.

– »›Spies and Gentlemen‹: The Birth of the British Spy Novel, 1893–1914«, in: *Victorian Studies* 24 (1980/81) S. 489–509.

Vester, Winfried, »The Theory of the Adventure Novel with Special Reference to John Buchan (*The Thirty-Nine Steps, Greenmantle, Mr Standfast*) and Robert Louis Stevenson (*Kidnapped*)«, unveröffentlichte Zulassungsarbeit für das Lehramt Universität Tübingen, 1984.

Wright, David, »The Great War, Government Propaganda and English ›Men of Letters‹ 1914–1916«, in: *Literature and History* 7 (Frühjahr 1978) S. 70–100.

Nachwort

Fiktionen eines »Scotsman on the Make«

I

> »Here was I, a very ordinary fellow, with no particular brains, and yet I was convinced that somehow I was needed to help this business through – that without me it would all go to blazes. I told myself it was sheer silly conceit, that four or five of the cleverest people living, with all the might of the British Empire at their back, had the job in hand. Yet I couldn't be convinced. It seemed as if a voice kept speaking in my ear, telling me to be up and doing, or I would never sleep again« (S. 145).

Oberflächlich betrachtet ist Richard Hannay nicht gerade der aufregendste Abenteurer, aber mehr als jeder andere Romanheld verkörpert er den Mann der Tat, der sich mit den Kräften der Unordnung messen muß. In *The Thirty-Nine Steps* (1915) trat er zum ersten Mal in Erscheinung und tauchte auch in anderen Thrillern von John Buchan auf – *Greenmantle* (1916), *Mr Standfast* (1919), *The Three Hostages* (1924) und *The Courts of the Morning* (1929) –, bis er den Stab einundzwanzig Jahre später in *The Island of Sheep* (1936) an eine jüngere Generation weitergab. Als Teil der populären Kultur erscheint dieser Held aus den Clubs der Londoner Gentlemen genauso archetypisch wie Gary Coopers Sheriff in *High Noon* (USA, 1952; dt. *Zwölf Uhr mittags*): Hannay, der das Schicksal ganzer Völker in der Hand hält; der im schottischen Hochmoor um sein Leben rennt; dessen Verfolger – Polizei, Deutsche oder wer sonst? – auf dem Bergkamm hinter ihm ausschwärmen, während ein Flugzeug am Himmel darüber seine Kreise zieht. Dieses Bild ist eine ebenso eindringliche Projektion der Problematik des modernen Menschen wie das von Winston Smith beim Anblick der Ratten in Zimmer 101. Doch im Gegensatz zu George Orwells *Nineteen Eighty-Four* (1949) ist es auf erheiternde, einfallsreiche und individualistische Weise auch irgendwie beruhigend. Ein Thriller kann entweder nach Schema F funktionieren oder aber Elementares aufzeigen; Buchan hatte sowohl die Begabung als auch den Ehrgeiz, seinen sturen, mit Common sense begabten Helden zu einem Odysseus des 20. Jahrhunderts werden zu lassen.

The Thirty-Nine Steps »von H de V« erschien erstmals in *Blackwood's Magazine* im Juni 1915, als britische Truppen auf dem Strand von Gallipoli festsaßen und die Russen in Galizien sich auf dem eiligen Rückzug vor den deutschen und österreichischen Streitkräften befanden. Der Roman war jedoch selbst zu diesem ungünstigen Zeitpunkt ein voller Erfolg. Die höchst einflußreiche literarische Zeitschrift *The British Weekly* mußte einräumen, daß ihre Rivalin *Blackwood's* »bis dahin nichts Besseres veröffentlicht hatte«:

> »We have everything here that can be wished – an excellent cipher story, with one or two points of novelty, a murder, a big subterranean business, a flight in a stolen motor-car, a monoplane floating with deadly intent, a Radical candidate, and all the rest. Not all the rest, for the woman has not yet appeared on the scene. But nobody must miss the tale«.[1]

Dieses Lob wurde dann etwas eingeschränkt, als *The British Weekly* herausfand, daß sich hinter H de V ein alter Gegner ihres eigenen Herausgebers, des Rev. William Robertson Nicoll, verbarg, aber bis dahin waren bereits 24 000 Exemplare der von *Blackwood's* am 19. Oktober 1915 veröffentlichten Erstausgabe verkauft. Nach über achtzig Jahren belaufen sich die Verkaufszahlen, die durch drei Filmadaptionen zusätzlich gesteigert wurden,[2] auf ungefähr 1 250 000 Exemplare. Der eigene Charakter der Filme, die sich seit Hitchcocks Version aus

1 *The British Weekly*, 1. Juli 1915, S. 287.

2 Vgl. Janet Adam Smith, *John Buchan: A Biography*, Oxford: Oxford University Press, 1985 ([1]1965), S. 197. Die erste Verfilmung stammt von Alfred Hitchcock aus dem Jahr 1935 mit Robert Donat als Hannay und dem

dem Jahre 1935 immer mehr von der Originalvorlage entfernten, deutet dabei auf die Besonderheit des Romans hin. Hier wurde ein klassischer Spionage-Thriller zugleich zur zutiefst persönlichen Aussage eines Mannes mit komplexem Charakter und einer unheimlich anmutenden prophetischen Gabe.

Anscheinend rein zufällig wird Hannay von dem todgeweihten Franklin Scudder als Kurier auserkoren, der der Regierung den Zeitplan für Armageddon übermitteln soll. Buchan, ein recht biederer Verleger aus Edinburgh, erlebte das Kriegsende als Staatssekretär des Informationsministeriums und befand sich damit im Zentrum des Geheimdiensts. Dabei war er teilweise verantwortlich für die Propagandaoffensive, welche zum Zerfall der deutschen Truppen beitrug. Als der letzte Hannay-Roman, *The Island of Sheep*, veröffentlicht wurde, war Buchan Generalgouverneur von Kanada; beim ersten war der Autor ebenso wie sein Held bestrebt, in die politischen Schaltstellen hineinzugelangen, an denen ein nicht besonders kompetenter Machtapparat mit der Katastrophe des totalen Krieges fertig werden mußte.

So erscheint beispielsweise die zu Anfang des vorliegenden Nachworts zitierte Passage einfach als ein Appell an individuelle Verantwortlichkeit zu einer Zeit, als die Kriegsmaschinerie Tausende von Menschen physisch vernichtete. Aber sie enthält auch Elemente aus John Bunyans *Pilgrim's Progress* (1678) und verschiedenen Shakespeare-Dramen, aus dem »inneren Licht« der Quäker und der »Bewußtseinsphilosophie« der schottischen Aufklärung des 18. Jahrhunderts. Der kanadische Historiker David Stafford bemerkt dazu:

Drehbuch von Ian Hay, dessen *First Hundred Thousand* ebenfalls 1915 in *Blackwood's* veröffentlicht wurde. Sie ist immer noch sehr sehenswert – mehr, als man von den nachfolgenden Produktionen sagen kann. Ralph Thomas produzierte 1960 eine Version mit Kenneth More, worüber *Halliwell's Film Guide* urteilt, sie sei »praktisch ein Handbuch, wie man einen Thriller nicht machen sollte«. Die 1978 von Don Sharp produzierte Version mit Robert Powell in der Hauptrolle spielt im Jahr 1914 – das einzige, worin ihre Handlung mit Buchans Roman übereinstimmt.

> »[...] within the bounds of a popular genre Buchan found not only a vehicle which would transport his readers to a land of romance and adventure, but maps to guide them on their secular pilgrimage through the tortuous ethical and social landscape of the early twentieth century [...]. They were sermons as well as yarns.«[3]

Angesichts von Gestalten wie Bullivant, dem freundlichen, jedoch selbstgefälligen Chef des britischen Amts für Aufklärung, der Scudders und Hannays Warnungen in den Wind schlägt, und Scudders Mörder, der mit den Plänen zur Mobilmachung im Kopf eiskalt aus einer Sitzung des Generalstabs der Alliierten hinausmarschiert, ist die Gabe der Propheten dringend vonnöten. Und selbst in den aufregendsten Momenten von *The Thirty-Nine Steps* ist die Kanzel der Scottish Free Kirk buchstäblich nie weit entfernt.

II

Oder behaupte ich damit etwa zuviel? »›It's all pure Rider Haggard and Conan Doyle‹« (S. 54), bemerkt der belesene Gastwirt und Möchtegern-Literaturkritiker, als Hannay mit Scudders Geschichte loslegt. »It's all pure William Le Queux and E. Phillips Oppenheim« hätte vielleicht nicht so gut geklungen, aber die Hunderte von billigen Thrillern, die von diesen beiden zwischen 1890 und 1914 produziert wurden, dienten Buchan augenscheinlich als Modell. 1913 nahm er die erste Version von *The Power House* (1916) in Angriff »to amuse myself writing a real shocker – a tribute at the shrine of my master in fiction – E. Phillips Oppenheim – the greatest Jewish writer since Isaiah«, wobei er jedoch mit ziemlicher Sicherheit einen anderen Juden im Sinn hatte.[4]

3 David T. Stafford, »John Buchan's Tales of Espionage: A Popular Archive of British History«, in: *Canadian Journal of History* 18 (1983), Heft 2, S. 4.

4 So Hugh Walpole; vgl. Smith, *John Buchan*, S. 178.

Der Polit-Thriller zielte in Großbritannien noch nie bloß auf spannende Unterhaltung. Die Aufmerksamkeit der Literaturkritik galt dabei insbesondere Autoren wie Graham Greene oder John le Carré. Doch die britische literarische Szene ist darüber hinaus ungewöhnlich reich an Themen wie Spionage und Intrigen, und sie zählt so untypische Vertreterinnen wie Anita Brookner oder Muriel Spark zu ihren Reihen. Dies ist gewiß zum Teil in den »puzzles« der Detektivgeschichte begründet, aber der »Schocker« – oder heute besser Polit-Thriller – entwickelte sich seit seiner Erfindung durch Benjamin Disraeli um 1840 parallel zum politischen Roman.[5]
Buchan war während seiner gesamten Laufbahn fasziniert von Disraeli, ohne freilich immer all dessen Taten gutzuheißen. Disraelis Roman *Sybil, or the Two Nations* (1845) weist alle wesentlichen Bestandteile eines Polit-Thrillers auf: das individuelle Drama – die Enterbung Egremonts und die mysteriöse Abstammung Sybils –, das nur durch ein politisches Drama aufgelöst werden kann – nämlich die Überwindung der Bedrohung durch den Chartismus der Arbeiterklasse –, die Intrige, die Unterwanderung durch eine Verschwörung sowie den blinden Zufall. Diese miteinander verflochtenen Begebenheiten gipfeln im Sturm der Chartisten und anarchistischen »Hellcats« auf Marney Castle. Inmitten einer Feuersbrunst und eines Gemetzels elisabethanischen Ausmaßes findet schließlich die Auflösung statt, durch die das britische Parteiensystem bestätigt wird. Das gibt dem Kritiker Jerry Palmer recht, der in *Thrillers* die Ansicht vertritt, das Genre trage im wesentlichen paranoide Züge: Der bedrohte Staat ist darin der beste aller Staaten; er wird dadurch, daß der Held ihn erfolgreich verteidigt, auf symbolische Weise neu begründet.[6] Ab 1840 verlor *Sybil* jedoch gegenüber Disraelis weniger bedrohlichem Roman *Coningsby* (1844) an Popularität, und das paranoide Grundmuster erwies sich seitdem als etwas

5 Vgl. Christopher Harvie, *The Centre of Things: Political Fiction in Britain from Disraeli to the Present*, London: Unwin Hyman, 1991, Kap. 1 und 3.
6 Siehe Jerry Palmer, *Thrillers*, London: Edward Arnold, 1978, S. 38.

überspannt. Es trat erst dann wieder auf, als ein friedfertiger Kapitalismus dem Krimkrieg und den Umbrüchen in Bismarcks Europa wich, und zwar in folgenden zwei Varianten: als »imaginäre Invasion«, deren Urform »The Battle of Dorking« von Colonel George Chesney (1877 in *Blackwood's* veröffentlicht) mit seiner Prophezeiung der Eroberung Großbritanniens durch die Deutschen darstellte, und als Roman beziehungsweise Drama einer Intrige an höherer Stelle, wie zum Beispiel Oscar Wildes *An Ideal Husband* (1893).[7] *The Thirty-Nine Steps* verknüpft beide Formen.

Ab 1880 revolutionierten neue Technologien – wie etwa Gewehre, raucharmes Pulver und Torpedos – die Kriegsführung, und in der Folge standen detaillierte Pläne zur Mobilmachung im Mittelpunkt der militärischen und marinestrategischen Programme der Großmächte. Dadurch erhielt die Spionage entscheidende Bedeutung, wie zum Beispiel die Dreyfus-Affäre zeigt, die Frankreich in zwei Lager spaltete. Die Romanfigur des Spions wurde zum Kassenschlager eines Genres, zu dessen typischen Vertretern Oppenheim und Le Queux, Conan Doyle und Edgar Wallace zählten.[8] Buchan hingegen schrieb auf einer höheren, aber nicht abgehobenen Ebene. Er vermied konsequent sowohl Femmes fatales – *The British Weekly* wartete vergebens auf ihr Erscheinen – als auch exotische Fremdenfeindlichkeit. Oppenheim war allerdings angeblich der Lieblingsautor von Arthur Balfour, Premierminister der Konservativen von 1900 bis 1905, dem *The Power House* gewidmet war und der zudem die Feststellung machte, daß ein Roman von Le Queux den Tories mindestens 10 000 Stimmen in jeder Wahl einbringen würde.[9] Solch ein intellektueller Ausflug in die Slums war nichts Einmaliges: um 1890 lobte so-

7 Vgl. dazu I. F. Clarke, *Voices Prophesying War*, London: Panther, 1969 ([1]1966), S. 30–47.

8 Vgl. David T. Stafford, »›Spies and Gentlemen‹: The Birth of the British Spy Novel, 1893–1914«, in: *Victorian Studies* 24 (1980/81) passim.

9 Vgl. Douglas Sladen, *Twenty Years of My Life*, London: Constable, 1915, S. 294.

gar der große Gladstone Marie Corellis lächerliche Melodramen als Versuch, den literarischen Geschmack der neuen Vorstädte zu bedienen.
Buchan orientierte sich teilweise an Oppenheim, indem er vornehmen Clubs und führenden Persönlichkeiten des Establishments beiläufig Achtung zollte – ein Moment der Irritation für Graham Greene.[10] Sein wahres literarisches Vorbild aber war Erskine Childers' Klassiker *The Riddle of the Sands*. Der 1903 veröffentlichte Roman handelt von deutschen Invasionsplänen, die von britischen Yachtseglern aufgedeckt werden, und wurde hunderttausendfach verkauft.[11] Am 19. August 1914 erkundigte sich Buchan in einem Brief an den Manager des Nelson-Verlags in Edinburgh, George Brown, nach den aktuellen Gesamtverkaufszahlen.[12] Wollte er es Childers' Roman denn etwa gleichtun? Buchan war ebenso ein Außenseiter wie der anglo-irische Republikaner; nach dessen Erschießung durch ein Exekutionskommando des irischen Freistaats schrieb er: »[. . .] no revolution ever produced a nobler or purer spirit«.
Neben dem Invasionsthema weisen die Romane beider weitere Parallelen auf. In jedem erhält die Hauptfigur – Childers' Carruthers und Buchans Hannay – überraschenden Besuch: Davies bzw. Scudder haben bereits den Großteil einer Verschwörung aufgedeckt. Die Enthüllung des wahren Sachverhalts aber folgt erst nach der Dekodierung zusammenhangloser Informationsfetzen; die Handlung selbst spielt sich auf einem Terrain ab, das dem Autor genau bekannt ist; der glückliche Ausgang der Sache erfordert ein Wettrennen gegen Fahrpläne, Gezeitentafeln und die Höchsten der hohen Politik. Childers war jedoch ebenso wie Kenneth Grahames Wasserratte in *The Wind in the Willows* (1908) fasziniert davon,

10 Vgl. Graham Greene, »The Last Buchan«, in: *The Lost Childhood and Other Essays*, Harmondsworth: Penguin, 1962 ([1]1951), S. 119.
11 Vgl. Clarke, *Voices Prophesying War*, S. 142 f.
12 Vgl. den Brief von Buchan an George Brown vom 19. August 1914 in: *Nelson and Company Letter Books*, Edinburgh University Library.

»sich in Booten herumzutreiben«. Daher braucht er doppelt so lange wie Buchan, um zur Sache zu kommen. Den Werken beider gemein ist wiederum die atmosphärische Dichte – etwas, das Le Queux und Oppenheim kaum jemals erreichten. Die kahlen Hügel von Tweedsmuir sind ebenso real wie die beengte Kajüte der *Dulcibella* oder die Sandbänke Borkums.

III

Wie gelangte Buchan dahin? David Daniell hat gewiß recht, wenn er in *The Thirty-Nine Steps* einen »Roman der Verwandlung« sieht – sowohl im Hinblick auf seinen Inhalt als auch auf seine Rolle für Buchans literarische Laufbahn.[13] Letztere war zu jener Zeit nicht gerade vielversprechend. Buchan war 1914 neununddreißig Jahre alt und hatte sich dem Genre des Thrillers erst im Jahre 1910 zugewandt. Im Zuge seiner Tätigkeit als gewissenhafter literarischer Berater eines renommierten und ambitionierten Verlages, der auf preiswerte Nachdrucke anspruchsvoller Werke spezialisiert war, geriet seine Karriere in eine gewisse Flaute.[14] Im Jahre 1913 wurde Buchans soeben erschienene Biographie eines Royalisten des 17. Jahrhunderts, *The Marquis of Montrose*, von zwei führenden schottischen Historikern aufs schärfste kritisiert, wobei der gnädigere von beiden zumindest die Handschrift »des brillanten Literaten eher als die des umsichtigen Historikers« erkennen konnte.[15] Was die Politik anbelangt, so hatte Buchans Zeitgenosse Winston Churchill bereits sechs Dienstjahre im Kabinett verbracht, derweil Buchan sich Peeblesshire warmhielt, einen fest in liberaler Hand befindlichen Wahlkreis, der ironischerweise von Sir Donald MacLean gehalten wurde, dem Vater eines

13 Vgl. David Daniell, »At the Foot of the Thirty-Ninth Step«, in: *The John Buchan Journal* 10 (Frühjahr 1991) S. 15–28.

14 Vgl. Allan Ramsay, *Nelson the Publisher* (1981), Abschnitt zit. in: *The John Buchan Journal* 4 (Herbst 1984) S. 10–14.

15 Vgl. Smith, *John Buchan*, S. 233.

späteren russischen Spions. Als gemäßigter Tory mit vielen Freunden unter den Liberalen war Buchan unglücklich über eine Partei, die den Ausbruch eines Bürgerkriegs in Irland geradezu provozierte.[16]

So lief er denn Gefahr, zum Ex-»Scotsman on the Make« zu werden. Seine Briefe weisen eher die Allwissenheit des fiktiven Hannay als jene Qualitäten auf, für die ihn Lawrence von Arabien den »great romancer of our blind and undeserving generation«[17] nannte. Folgende an George Blackwood gerichteten Worte klingen allzu übertrieben:

> »I am compelled to write you a letter to congratulate you on the exceeding excellence of ›Maga‹. It is out of doubt the best magazine of the day but better than I think it has ever been in its long history. It was natural that in time of war ›Maga‹ should be good but that it should be so damned good is not natural. Art and brains come in there and I congratulate you most sincerely.«[18]

»The Government has got the bullet in them all right. They may run for a bit, but they are bound to come down soon.« Diese Weisheit würde Buchan natürlich nicht an Freunde weitergeben, die Mitglieder der Regierung waren, wie beispielsweise sein Gönner Lord Chancellor Haldane oder Raymond Asquith, der Sohn des Premierministers.[19] Er gehörte auch nicht zu jenen Literaten, dem andere Mitglieder dieser Gattung über den Weg trauten. In Ford Madox Fords Tetralogie *Parade's End* (1924–28) arbeitet Vincent MacMaster, ein ehrgeiziger, schottischer Beamter aus einer Kleinstadt in Fife,

16 Vgl. Christopher Harvie, »Second Thoughts of a Scotsman on the Make: Politics, Nationalism and Myth in John Buchan«, in: *The Scottish Historical Review* 70 (April 1991), Heft 188, S. 34.

17 T. E. Lawrence in einem Brief an Edward Garnett vom 1. August 1933; in: T. E. Lawrence, *The Letters*, hrsg. von David Garnett, London: Cape, 1938, S. 772.

18 Brief an George Blackwood vom 2. April 1915; in: *William Blackwood and Sons' Letterbooks*, National Library of Scotland, Mss. Nr. 30170, 30353 und 30402.

19 Vgl. ebd. den Brief an Blackwood vom 27. März 1914.

sich im Dienste der Regierung während des Krieges hoch, was auf Kosten des intelligenten, unbestechlichen englischen Torys Christopher Tietjens geschieht. Ein feindseliges Porträt von Buchan etwa? Sowohl Ford als auch dessen Freund Joseph Conrad schrieben ihm das Image eines Karrieremachers zu – ein Ruf, der ebenso hartnäckig haftet wie Buchans angeblicher Antisemitismus.

Im Herbst 1914 waren Buchans Aktivitäten mehr aufs Geschäftliche als auf patriotische Ziele konzentriert. Er gehörte nicht wie H. G. Wells oder Thomas Hardy zu jenen liberalen Intellektuellen, die scharenweise zum Sonderamt für Propaganda strömten, das Charles Masterman, Buchans angeheirateter Cousin, in Wellington House eingerichtet hatte.[20] Vielmehr war er erfolgreich bemüht, das Überleben des Verlags Nelson's zu sichern. Das bewerkstelligte er zum einen mit der Vorstellung von *Nelson's History of the War*, für die er auch als Verfasser verantwortlich zeichnete – der erste Teil erschien im März 1915 –, zum anderen mit der Geschäftsübernahme des Leipziger Paperback-Verlags Tauchnitz im Gebiet der Alliierten.[21] Daneben arbeitete Buchan für Blackwood's, seinen Nachbarn in der Londoner Paternoster Row, als Autor – fest entschlossen, aus dem Thriller Kapital zu schlagen. Angesichts des um sich greifenden Patriotismus wirken diese Aktivitäten ein wenig ichbezogen, auch wenn das dem typischen Verhalten der meisten schottischen Geschäftsleute in der damaligen Zeit entsprach, die sich von der Beeinträchtigung des Handels mehr betroffen fühlten als von der Aussicht auf den totalen Krieg.[22]

20 Vgl. David Wright, »The Great War, Government Propaganda and English ›Men of Letters‹ 1914–1916«, in: *Literature and History* 7 (Frühjahr 1978) S. 70–100.

21 Vgl. die Briefe an George Brown vom 22. Dezember 1914, 4. und 7. Januar 1915 in *Nelson Letter Books* sowie Keith Grieves, »Nelson's History of the War: John Buchan as a Contemporary Military Historian, 1915–22«, unveröffentlichter Vortrag vor der Social History Society 1991, passim.

22 Vgl. Christopher Harvie, *No Gods and Precious Few Heroes: Scotland since 1914*, Edinburgh: Edinburgh University Press, 1993 ([1]1981), S. 12 bis 15.

Den Übergang vom historischen Roman nach Stevensons Vorbild zum zeitgenössischen Thriller markiert Buchans Roman *Prester John*, der 1910 unter dem Titel *The Black General* als Fortsetzungsgeschichte in *The Captain*, einer Wochenzeitschrift für Jungen, erschien. Dieses Werk weist jedoch einige Unstimmigkeiten auf: sein Held, David Crawfurd, ist zu selbstzufrieden und dessen Hund zu einfallsreich; die beiden nehmen sich wie Tim und Struppi aus, während der afrikanische Rebell John Laputa eher Othello gleicht. Der Erfolg des Romans festigte jedoch Buchans Beziehung zu George Blackwood, für den er eine Biographie des schottischen Richters Andrew Jameson Lord Ardwall verfaßte, und führte 1913 schließlich zur Veröffentlichung von *The Power House*, einem Roman, den Buchan zur Aufmunterung des erkrankten Arthur Balfour schrieb. Blackwood begrüßte das Buch – »Readers will get something that they do not perhaps altogether expect from your pen [...]«[23] – und hoffte, mehr davon zu bekommen. Der Schriftverkehr zwischen Buchan und Blackwood war jedoch bis zum 7. Dezember 1914 unterbrochen. An diesem Tag schrieb Buchan:

> »I was sent to bed by the doctor five weeks ago to avoid an operation and I am glad to say I think I have managed it. I have amused myself in bed with writing a shocker of the type of *The Power House*, only more so [...]. It has certainly the merit of what is called topical interest.«[24]

Er legte ein Manuskript mit dem Titel *The Black Stone* bei. Blackwood »approved of it right up to the end [...]. The story is really thrilling«, und er riet Buchan (Gott sei Dank!) davon ab, den Titel in *The Kennels of War* umzuändern. Bis zum 28. Januar des folgenden Jahres hatten beide sich auf *The Thirty-Nine Steps* geeinigt.[25] Der Einfluß von George Black-

23 Brief von Blackwood an Buchan vom 17. Oktober 1913 in *Blackwood Letterbooks*.

24 Brief vom 7. Dezember 1914 ebd.

25 Vgl. ebd. Brief von Blackwood an Buchan vom 28. Januar 1915.

wood zeigt sich beispielsweise darin, daß Hannay auf seiner Reise nach Schottland das Land der Ardwalls durchquert; außerdem scheint Appleton, der Kopf des Black Stone, ein Verwandter von Andrew Lumley, dem überintelligenten Bösewicht aus *The Power House*, zu sein, der wiederum dem für seine Kaltblütigkeit berüchtigten Balfour ähnelt. Blackwood wußte jedoch nichts von Buchans literarischen Machenschaften bei Nelson's, dessen Mitarbeiter auf den Thriller von H de V erst aufmerksam wurden, als Buchan die Buchversion dem Chef des Verlagsunternehmens, Tommy Nelson, widmete.

Buchan gab an, daß er das Buch in Ermangelung eines besseren Vorhabens geschrieben hätte. Aus der Korrespondenz mit Nelson's geht hervor, daß er an einem Zwölffingerdarmgeschwür litt und am 23. Oktober von Sir Bertrand Dawson ins Bett verwiesen wurde. Dawson riet »either an operation which is a fairly drastic one, or complete rest for six or seven weeks.«[26] Nichtsdestotrotz war Buchan zwei Wochen später wieder auf den Beinen und ging ins Büro. Auch wenn es lediglich Indizienbeweise für die folgende Annahme gibt, da die offiziellen Dokumente bis heute nicht eingesehen werden können, so meine ich doch, daß Buchans geschäftliche Inanspruchnahme, seine Erkrankung und seine Abwesenheit vom Treiben in Wellington House in erster Linie zur Tarnung dienten. Buchan, der Verleger, deckte bereits Buchan, den Geheimagenten – eine Rolle, die in *The Thirty-Nine Steps* vorsichtig angedeutet wird.

Kurz nach der Kriegserklärung wurde Buchan zu Sir Edward Grey ins Außenministerium vorgeladen. Am 18. November erwähnt er ein Treffen mit dem Herausgeber der *Times* und berichtet von alarmierendem Gerede über »tremendous preparations being made for the invasion of the English coast which is expected any day this week. The Southern Command is entirely depleted of all troops.«[27] Warum dieser schnelle

26 Brief von Buchan an George Brown vom 23. Oktober 1914 in *Nelson Letter Books*.

27 Brief von Buchan an Brown vom 18. November 1914 ebd.

Wechsel zur politischen Mitte? Buchans *History of the War* war offenbar bedeutsam; um dem Vorwurf, das Werk sei propagandistisch, zu entgehen, mußte ihr Verfasser offizielle Publicity vermeiden. Buchans gemäßigt-konservative politische Linie kam ihm dabei vermutlich zu Hilfe. Angesichts eines drohenden Bürgerkriegs in Großbritannien blieb er Liberalen wie Grey, Masterman und Haldane, dem stellvertretenden Kriegsminister, freundlich gesonnen. Die Regierung konnte auf die liberalen Literaten zählen, sorgte sich jedoch um konservative Zwangsvorstellungen bezüglich ausländischer Spione, Verräter unter den Liberalen und dergleichen mehr. Solche anscheinend »spontan« verfaßten Propagandastreiche wie Rupert Brookes Sonett-Sequenz »The Soldier« (1915), Ian Hays Roman *The First Hundred Thousand* aus demselben Jahr, der wie *The Thirty-Nine Steps* zuerst in *Blackwood's Magazine* als Fortsetzungsgeschichte erschien, und Buchans Werk lassen »a big subterranean movement going on« (S. 11) vermuten, von der Buchan selbst ein wichtiger Teil war.[28]

Das entscheidende Element von *The Thirty-Nine Steps* besteht möglicherweise in seinem zentralen Rätsel, Scudders »little black pocket-book« mit den geheimnisvollen Codewörtern »›Hofgaard‹, ›Luneville‹, [. . .] ›Avocado‹ [. . .] and [. . .] ›Pavia‹« (S. 38) einerseits und der abwesenden Heldin Julia Czechenyi andererseits. Um den Code zu entschlüsseln, muß Hannay eingestehen, daß er alles andere als »a very ordinary fellow« ist, sondern früher für den geheimen Nachrichtendienst in Südafrika gearbeitet hat. Auch Buchan hatte sich in seiner Eigenschaft als Privatsekretär von Sir Alfred Milner, dem Generalgouverneur in Kapstadt, mit der Verwendung einfacher, aus der Römerzeit stammender und als »Julius-Cäsar-Zahlen« bezeichneter »monoalphabetischer Ziffern« befaßt; er könnte aber auch im Verlauf seiner historischen Studien der Antike darauf gestoßen sein. Besagte Ziffernart war

28 Vgl. J. W. H. de l'A. Buchan, »John Buchan and the Great War«, in: *The John Buchan Journal* 7 (Winter 1987) S. 2–9.

1914, als Sir Alfred Ewing, Professor in Cambridge und Direktor der Marineakademie, zur Admiralität beordert wurde, um zusammen mit Admiral Reginald Hall die später als »Room 40« bekanntgewordene Abteilung für Dekodierung einzurichten, immer noch allgemein gebräuchlich. Ewing war wie Buchan der Sohn eines Pfarrers der Scottish Free Kirk. Was lag also für ihn und den Außenminister näher, als Buchan, der über leidliche Deutschkenntnisse verfügte und sich überdies in der deutschen Politik gut auskannte, mit der Assistenz bei der Interpretation der ersten Dekodierungen zu beauftragen?[29]

Diese Umstände erklären nicht nur das Treffen mit Grey, sondern auch den Respekt, den der amerikanische Agent Blenkiron in *Greenmantle* für den Marinenachrichtendienst hegt.[30] Wie Blenkiron setzt auch Buchan gern das Mittel des »double-bluff« ein, was sich beispielsweise in der Akribie zeigt, mit der versucht wird, Scudders ein wenig altertümlich anmutenden Code zu knacken. Ist *The Thirty-Nine Steps* in Wahrheit vielleicht ein raffinierter Versuch, die Deutschen über den Wissensstand der Admiralität bezüglich der Dekodiermöglichkeiten in die Irre zu führen? Bis zum Jahr 1915 waren den Briten Ausgaben der drei wichtigsten, von der deutschen Admiralität noch bis 1917 benutzten Codebücher in die Hände gefallen. Und schließlich ist auch Mr. Appleton, der kahlköpfige Archäologe, »›[who] could hood bis eyes like a hawk‹« (S. 104), ein anschauliches Beispiel für das Mittel des »double-bluff«:

> »There was something weird and devilish in these eyes, cold, malignant, unearthly and most hellishly clever. They fascinated me like the bright eyes of a snake. I had a strong impulse to throw myself on his mercy and offer to join his side [. . .]« (S. 108).

29 Vgl. Patrick Beesly, *Room 40: British Naval Intelligence, 1914–1918*, Oxford: Oxford University Press, 1982, S. 1–30.

30 Vgl. J. Buchan, *Greenmantle*, London: Hodder and Stoughton, 1916, S. 155.

Buchan, der bereits Andrew Lumley nach dem Vorbild von Arthur Balfour geschaffen hatte, fiel es nicht schwer, die Figur des Mr. Appleton zu ersinnen. Man vergleiche die obige Passage mit der Beschreibung von Admiral Hall, dem Chef des Room 40, im *Dictionary of National Biography*:

> »[Germans] who had failed to respond to ordinary interrogation often became as putty in his hands. There was a hypnotic power about his glance which broke their resistance. On occasion his manner became explosive, and the facial twitch, which gave him the name of ›Blinker‹ became exaggerated [. . .].«[31]

Ebenso Admiral William James' Bemerkung: »Such eyes as the man has!«[32]

IV

Buchans offizielle Kontakte liefern möglicherweise eine Erklärung dafür, warum er Hannay nach der Entdeckung von Scudders Leiche in Richtung Norden fliehen läßt. In einer Großstadt kann ein Flüchtiger spurlos verschwinden; im Hochmoor von Galloway dagegen ist er auf Gedeih und Verderb ausgeliefert. Wollte Buchan den Höhepunkt des Thrillers ursprünglich in der näheren Umgebung des neuen Marinestützpunkts im schottischen Rosyth ansiedeln? Die Vorstellung von einem plötzlichen vernichtenden Angriff auf die Grand Fleet hatte bereits 1906 in *The Invasion of 1911* von Le Queux und H. W. Wilson, dem Marinekorrespondenten der *Daily Mail*, Ausdruck gefunden, und eine derartige Bedrohung könnte einen Grund für Hannays Reise abgegeben haben. (Hitchcock muß zu diesem Zweck Miss Smith einsetzen,

31 William James, »Admiral Sir (William) Reginald Hall«, in: *Dictionary of National Biography*, Oxford: Oxford University Press, 1959.
32 William James, *The Eyes of the Navy*, London: Methuen, 1955, S. 1.

die tot in Hannays Bett fällt und hilfreicherweise eine Landkarte umklammert hält, auf welcher ein Teil von Schottland zu sehen ist.) Wenn Buchan aber die Idee eines schottischen Schauplatzes im Hinterkopf hatte, so wurde er gewiß von Masterman oder seinen sonstigen Kontaktpersonen in Whitehall davor gewarnt, sie umzusetzen. Denn Rosyth war nicht nur eine streng geheime Angelegenheit; die ersten Kriegswochen brachten ein weiteres großes Geheimnis mit sich, das für schlechtes Gewissen sorgte. Der Super-Dreadnought *Audacious* war wegen eines drohenden U-Boot-Angriffs zusammen mit der Grand Fleet nach Rosyth abbeordert worden, sah sich jedoch aufgrund fehlender Verteidigungsmittel gezwungen, Scapa Flow auf den Orkney-Inseln wieder zu verlassen. Am 27. Oktober 1914 geriet er in ein deutsches Minenfeld und sank vor der Küste der irischen Provinz Ulster. Obwohl er sich für jedermann sichtbar in Küstennähe befand, wurde der Verlust erst nach dem Waffenstillstand im Jahr 1918 bekanntgegeben. Die mysteriösen Aufklärungsflugzeuge, auf die Buchan möglicherweise von seinen Verbindungsleuten in Galloway aufmerksam gemacht wurde, waren mit ziemlicher Sicherheit keine Deutschen, sondern blieben mysteriös, da sie in Zusammenhang mit diesem Unglück standen.[33]

Aber es gibt noch andere aus dem Zeitgeist der Mittelklasse resultierende Gründe für Hannays Wanderschaft: den Reiz der offenen Landstraße, der in vielen Werken der »schönen Literatur« gepriesen wurde, wie beispielsweise in Buchans *Scholar Gipsies* (1898), die Nachwirkung von Baden-Powells *Scouting for Boys* (1908), vor allem aber den Einfluß von Robert Louis Stevenson. Kaum zwanzig Jahre nach seinem Tod verkörperte gerade dieser Schriftsteller in den Augen von Literaten wie Sir Walter Raleigh und Sir Arthur Quiller-Couch, die ihrerseits eifrig bedacht waren, die deutsche Wissenschaft aus den Lehrplänen von Oxford und Cambridge zu verdrän-

33 Vgl. D. Daniell, »That Infernal Aeroplane«, in: *The John Buchan Journal* 11 (Frühjahr 1992) passim.

gen,[34] sowohl künstlerischen Scharfblick als auch männliche Individualität. Die bedeutsame Herausforderung, die Alan Breck in *Kidnapped* (1886) an David Balfour richtet – der im selben Boot sitzt wie Hannay –, klingt in dem gesamten Roman an:

»›Ye maun lie bare and hard, and brook many an empty belly. Your bed shall be the moorcock's, and your life shall be like the hunted deer's, and ye shall sleep with your hand on your weapons. Ay, man, ye shall taigle many a weary foot, or we get clear! I tell ye this at the start, for it's a life I ken well. But if ye ask what other chance ye have, I answer: Nane. Either take to the heather with me, or else hang.‹«[35]

Auch Buchans Werke weisen stets eine gewisse didaktische Komponente auf, und Hannays »veldcraft« erscheint sogar unter rein praktischen Gesichtspunkten recht nützlich für neue Subalternoffiziere: unter der Horizontlinie bleiben, durchs Niemandsland kriechen, nach Stolperdrähten Ausschau halten – alles vernünftige Ratschläge, verglichen mit den abgehobenen Militärakademie-Vorstellungen, die von vielen Berufsoffizieren gehegt wurden.

Wenn wir Hannays Reiseroute betrachten, ergibt sich jedoch eine eher philosophische Grundlage. Buchans diesbezügliche Verweise sind so rätselhaft wie Scudders Notizen über den Black Stone. Es werden lediglich sechs reale schottische Ortsbezeichnungen genannt: Dumfries, die Flüsse Cairn, Tweed und Deuch, sowie Cairnsmore of Fleet und Moffat. Allerdings gibt es genügend andere Hinweise für die Leser, um relativ genau zu ermitteln, wo Hannay unterwegs ist.[36]

34 Vgl. C. Harvie, »The Politics of Stevenson«, in: Chris Baldick (Hrsg.), *The Social Mission of English Criticism*, Oxford: Oxford University Press, 1981, S. 110.

35 Robert Louis Stevenson, *Kidnapped*, London: Cassell, 1886, S. 165.

36 J. A. Paterson und W. M. Russell Paterson versuchen in ihrem Aufsatz »The Thirty-Nine Steps« in: *The John Buchan Journal* 7 (Winter 1987)

Auch für einen Wanderer oder Radfahrer wäre es bestimmt sehr interessant, der Spur des Fliehenden zu folgen. Hannay beginnt seine Tour am längst stillgelegten Bahnhof von Gatehouse of Fleet am Nachmittag des 25. Mai und wandert am Berg Cairnsmore of Fleet entlang nach Creetown. Am nächsten Tag fährt er denselben Weg zurück und springt etwa sieben Kilometer vor Dumfries vom Zug. Dann schlägt er den Weg nach Norden zur A 712, der Straße von Newton Stewart nach New Galloway, ein. Die Szene mit dem belesenen Gastwirt am 27. und 28. Mai spielt nördlich von New Galloway an der A 713; Hannays erster Autodiebstahl führt ihn erst über die B 759 durch Moniaive, dann über die A 702 durch Thornhill und schließlich über den Dalveen-Paß ins Tal des Clyde. Bei Moffat verunglückt er mit dem Auto, in Lockerbie (Brattleburn) hält er seine Rede vor der politischen Versammlung, zu der ihn der Kandidat der Radikalen geladen hat. Am 29. Mai radelt er, von Sir Harry mit einer Landkarte ausgestattet, die Straßenkuppe bei Tweedhopefoot hinauf, wo er sich als Ecky Turnbull, der Straßenarbeiter, ausgibt und Marmaduke Jopleys Auto an sich bringt. Zusammen mit Jopley fährt er nach Norden in die Gemeinde von Broughton und setzt seinen Insassen am Broughton Place aus. Daraus folgt, daß das Zusammentreffen mit dem kahlköpfigen Archäologen am 30. Mai in der Gegend des Nordhangs der Broughton Heights stattfindet, von wo aus der Firth of Forth in der Ferne zu sehen ist. Danach führt ein nächtlicher Spurt Hannay zurück zu Turnbulls Cottage. Seine Malaria-Attacke dauert bis zum 12. Juni; im Anschluß daran geht er zu Fuß nach Moffat und nimmt von Beattock Junction den Zug nach Süden.

Ist diese Route von Bedeutung? Sie hat weder etwas mit Karolides noch mit den Plänen der Admiralität zu tun und endet außerdem in einem zwölftägigen Halbkoma, das verdächtig

S. 14–19, Hannays Route durch Südschottland zu rekonstruieren. Ich stimme weitgehend mit ihnen überein, würde allerdings die Szene mit dem kahlköpfigen Archäologen etwa sechs Meilen nordwestlich des angenommenen Ortes ansiedeln.

nach Zeitschinderei aussieht. Und dennoch hat Hannays schottische Pilgerreise dieselbe Funktion wie Davies' und Carruthers' Segeltörn vor der Küste Frieslands. Sie stiftet einen Ortssinn und stellt so einen Bezugsrahmen für all die literarischen und topographischen Verweise her, die ein Gefühl der Bedrohung und des Schicksalskampfes vermitteln: Ein Konflikt steht bevor, in dem über individuelles und nationales Geschick entschieden werden soll.

David Daniell lokalisiert diese »Verwandlung« im Gasthaus von Galloway, wo der junge Wirt bei Hannays Ankunft eine Stelle aus dem zweiten Buch von John Miltons *Paradise Lost* (1667) zitiert:

> »As when a Gryphon through the wilderness
> With wingéd step, o'er hill and moory dale
> Pursues the Arimaspian« (S. 51).

Hannay fungiert als goldraubender Arimaspianer, und der Greif – oder auch Luzifer – verkörpert den »gefallenen Engel« Deutschland, in dessen kulturellem Umfeld Buchan einen Großteil seiner Ausbildung erhielt. Auf diesem Hintergrund stellt sich Hannays Konfrontation mit der Gruppe des Black Stone auf dem Hochmoor Südschottlands als eine zeitgemäße Neuformulierung der calvinistischen Konfrontation mit den Mächten der Dunkelheit dar, auf die eine Erneuerung folgt – sie ist, kurz gesagt, ein auf die Ursachen des Krieges verweisender »Schöpfungsmythos«.[37]

Die Landschaft der Borders-Region, in der sich Buchan wie in seiner Westentasche auskannte, wurde in der calvinistischen Geschichte hochgeschätzt. Sie hatte schon den Covenanters, den radikalen Presbyterianern Schottlands, in den »Killing Times« um 1680 Schutz geboten. Buchan hat die Borders-Region bereits in drei früheren Romanen geschildert – *Sir Quixote of the Moors* (1895), *John Burnet of Barns* (1898) und *A Lost Lady of Old Years* (1899). Im ersten reitet Sieur de Ro-

37 Vgl. Daniell, »At the Foot of the Thirty-Ninth Step«, S. 20.

hanne, der auch in *John Burnet* auftaucht, »blind« durch die Lowther Hills zum Tal des Clyde; der zweite spielt gleichfalls während der »Killing Times« und zeichnet die Topographie Schottlands sehr präzise nach. Burnet, der von seinem bösen Cousin Gilbert erst als Rebell der Covenanters verdingt und danach verfolgt wird, befindet sich in der gleichen Situation wie Hannay. Er ist gezwungen, im Tal des Upper Tweed – mit der Obrigkeit und Gilbert auf den Fersen – Zeit zu schinden. Im letztgenannten Roman, der in den Jahren 1745/46 spielt, agiert Francis Birkenshaw, einer der unsympathischsten Helden von John Buchan, im Dienste der Jakobitin Mrs. Murray of Broughton. Nach einem ausgedehnten Koma kommt er – zu spät – zur Schlacht von Culloden, in der die Sache der Jakobiten ihr entscheidendes Ende nahm.
Tatsächlich aber findet praktisch die gesamte Handlung von *The Thirty-Nine Steps* vor Buchans eigener Haustür statt. Scudder wird am Portland Place ermordet, also ganz in der Nähe von Buchans Londoner Behausung. Hannay beginnt seine Schottlandreise nahe beim Hofgut der Ardwalls; Broughton war früher die Gemeinde von Buchans Vater, wo in der Free Kirk – dem jetzigen John-Buchan-Museum – eine Fensterscheibe der Hannay-Familie gewidmet ist. Die militärische Unterredung, bei welcher der falsche Lord Alloa die Dokumente an sich bringt, findet im Haus von Lord Haldane in Queen Anne's Gate statt; die entscheidende Konfrontation mit dem Black Stone erfolgt auf dem Grund und Boden der Ferienvilla der Buchans in Broadstairs. Gerade so wie John Bunyan die Topographie Bedfordshires in sein Versepos *The Pilgrim's Progress* einfügt und Orwell seinen Roman *1984* mit dem Satz »It was a bright, cold day in April, and the clocks were striking thirteen«[38] beginnen läßt, erzielt Buchan eine Schauerwirkung, indem er das Vertraute und das Beängstigende nebeneinanderstellt. Er läßt überdies Hannay auf Figu-

38 George Orwell, *Nineteen Eighty-Four*, London: Secker and Warburg, 1949, S. 1.

James Joyce: *Dubliners.* A Selection. 104 S. UB 9181 – *Penelope.* The Last Chapter of »Ulysses«. 191 S. UB 9243

Rudyard Kipling: *The Jungle Book.* 219 S. UB 9244

D. H. Lawrence: *The Fox.* 135 S. UB 9209

John le Carré: *Call for the Dead.* 240 S. UB 9048

Doris Lessing: *Three African Stories.* 77 S. UB 9245 – *To Room Nineteen.* 72 S. UB 9151

Katherine Mansfield: *The Garden-Party.* Five Short Stories. 85 S. UB 9152

W. Somerset Maugham: *The Letter.* 75 S. UB 9183

A. A. Milne: *Winnie-the-Pooh.* Ill. 180 S. UB 9231

Liam O'Flaherty: *A Tourist's Guide to Ireland.* 101 S. UB 9272

George Orwell: *England Your England and Other Essays.* 122 S. UB 9024

Rosamunde Pilcher: *Snow in April.* 262 S. UB 9017

Alan Sillitoe: *The Loneliness of the Long-distance Runner.* 88 S. UB 9192 – *Saturday Night and Sunday Morning.* 360 S. UB 9038

Muriel Spark: *The Prime of Miss Jean Brodie.* 189 S. UB 9193

Robert Louis Stevenson: *The Bottle Imp.* 59 S. UB 9157 – *The Strange Case of Dr. Jekyll and Mr. Hyde.* 119 S. UB 9167 – *Treasure Island.* Ill. 334 S. UB 9258

Jonathan Swift: *Gulliver's Travels.* Part I: A Voyage to Lilliput. 159 S. UB 9274

J. R. R. Tolkien: *Farmer Giles of Ham.* Ill. 112 S. UB 9025

Evelyn Waugh: *The Loved One.* 192 S. UB 9233

Fay Weldon: *The Fat Woman's Joke.* 216 S. UB 9028

H. G. Wells: *The Invisible Man.* 270 S. UB 9013 – *The Time Machine.* 160 S. UB 9176

Oscar Wilde: *The Canterville Ghost.* 64 S. UB 9177 – *The Happy Prince and Other Tales.* 91 S. UB 9293 – *The Picture of Dorian Gray.* 344 S. UB 9019

Virginia Woolf: *Mrs Dalloway's Party.* A Short Story Sequence. 93 S. UB 9196

Philipp Reclam jun. Stuttgart

Fremdsprachentexte

IN RECLAMS UNIVERSAL-BIBLIOTHEK

Englische und amerikanische Dramen

Auswahl

Samuel Beckett: Waiting for Godot. 147 S. UB 9214
Brendan Behan: The Hostage. 141 S. UB 9222
Edward Bond: Summer. 104 S. UB 9197
John Gay: The Beggar's Opera. 143 S. UB 9228
Arthur Miller: The Crucible. 224 S. UB 9257 – Death of a Salesman. 171 S. UB 9172
Eugene O'Neill: Long Day's Journey into Night. 216 S. UB 9252
John Osborne: The Entertainer. 143 S. UB 9191
J. B. Priestley: An Inspector Calls. 117 S. UB 9218
Willy Russell: Educating Rita. 132 S. UB 9040
Peter Shaffer: Amadeus. 199 S. UB 9219
William Shakespeare: Hamlet. 261 S. UB 9292 – Macbeth. 167 S. UB 9220 – A Midsummer Night's Dream. 160 S. UB 9247 – Romeo and Juliet. 219 S. UB 9005
Bernard Shaw: Mrs Warren's Profession. 198 S. UB 9166 – Pygmalion. 197 S. UB 9266
Tom Stoppard: Rosencrantz and Guildenstern are Dead. 171 S. UB 9185
John Millington Synge: The Playboy of the Western World. 128 S. UB 9211
Oscar Wilde: The Importance of Being Earnest. 141 S. UB 9267 – Lady Windermere's Fan. 101 S. UB 9187
Thornton Wilder: Our Town. 127 S. UB 9168
Tennessee Williams: Cat on a Hot Tin Roof. 224 S. UB 9039 – The Glass Menagerie. 149 S. UB 9178 – A Streetcar Named Desire. 199 S. UB 9240

Philipp Reclam jun. Stuttgart